GOOD GARB

Dear Dr. Kennedy,
To a truly wonderful man —
Thank you for all your
generosity.
Best Wishes,
Laura + Bill

A Practical Guide to Practical Clothing

WILLIAM DASHEFF and GOOD GARB LAURA DEARBORN

◭ A Delta Book

Published by
Dell Publishing Co., Inc.
1 Dag Hammarskjold Plaza
New York, New York 10017

Delta ® TM 755118, Dell Publishing Co., Inc.

Printed in the United States of America

First printing—November 1980

Designed by Hermann Strohbach

Drawings by Susan Haskins

Library of Congress Cataloging in Publication Data

Dasheff, William, 1950–
    Good garb.

    (A Delta book)
    Includes index.
    1.   Clothing and dress.   I.   Dearborn, Laura,
1951–   joint author.   II.   Title.
TX340.D37   646'.3   80-21873

ISBN: 0-440-52588-8

Author's Note:

If you have any comments, criticisms, suggestions, or interesting
companies to recommend, we'd love to hear from you. Write:

Dasheff and Dearborn
GOOD GARB
c/o Dell Publishing Co., Inc.
245 East 47th Street
New York, N.Y. 10017

Acorn Products Company, 6-92; **Alden Shoe Company**, 6-79, 80, 81; **Allen Edmonds**, 6-65, 66, 67, 68; **Banana Equipment**, 5-55; **Eddie Bauer**, 4-12, 13, 17, 21, 22; 5-4, 17, 18, 27, 28, 29, 62, 63, 64, 65, 66, 67, 94, 95, 96; 6-15, 34, 36, 47, 48, 49, 51, 52; **L.L. Bean**, 4-15, 60; 5-40, 43, 83, 91, 92, 100, 105, 109; 6-18, 19, 20, 21, 53; **Bergman Company**, 4-35; **Birkenstock**, 6-63, 64; **Bladen Bros**, 4-57; **Brigade Quartermaster**, 4-51; 5-24, 72, 86; **Cambrian Fly Fishers**, 4-62, 63, 64, 65, 66; 5-30; **Camp**, 7, 5-52, 53, 54, 71; **Canor Plarex**, 5-75; 6-89; **Chippewa**, 6-83, 84, 85, 86, 87, 88; **Adam Cogneato**, 4-7, 19, 33, 54, 60; 5-26, 50, 51, 69, 78; 6-82, 91; **Country Store of Concord**, 5-32; **Danner Shoes**, 6-35, 37, 38; **Duofold**, 4-8, 72, 73; **Early Winters**, 4-9, 20; 5-84, 85; **Flight Suits Ltd.**, 4-67, 68, 69, 70; **French Creek**, 4-32, 33, 34, 54; 5-5, 23, 33, 34, 36, 37, 38, 39, 87, 88, 89, 90; **Gokeys**, 5-11, 12, 13, 82, 108; 6-22; **Great Pacific Ironworks**, 4-27, 28, 29; 5-31; **Henri-Lloyd**, 5-74; **Joseph M. Herman**, 6-25, 26, 27, 28; **Huc**, 5-47, 48, 49; **Kalpakian Knitting Mills**, 4-49; **Komito Boots**, 6-6, 7, 8, 9; **Peter Limmer and Sons**, 6-10; **Line**, 7, 5-73; **Lucchese**, 6-41, 42, 43, 44, 45; **Marmot Mountain Works**, 5-56, 57, 58, 59, 70, 77; **Randal Merrell**, 6-1, 2, 3, 4, 5; **Miller Shoes**, 6-54, 55, 56, 57, 58, 59, 60, 61, 62; **David Morgan**, 4-1, 2, 3, 4, 5, 6, 22, 36, 37, 38; 5-101, 102, 103, 104, 111; **Nocona Boots**, 6-69, 70, 71, 72, 73; **Norm Thompson**, 4-11, 23, 24, 25, 42, 43, 44, 53, 55, 56, 71; 5-3, 6, 7, 14, 15, 20, 21, 41, 42, 45, 46, 93, 99, 106, 107; **Norsewear**, 4-50; **Northface**, 5-61; **Orvis**, 4-14, 26, 39, 40, 41, 59, 75, 61; 5-1, 2, 16, 19, 44, 79, 80, 81, 97, 98; 6-33, 50, 70; **Redwing**, 6-23, 24; **REI**, 5-76; **Robbins Mountaingear/Mountainwear**, 4-45, 46, 47, 48; **Rugged Wear Ltd.**, 4-7; **W.C. Russell**, 6-29, 30, 31, 32; **Sebago**, 6-77, 78; **The Ski Hut**, 4-10, 16, 30, 74; 5-60; **Milt Sparks Belts**, 5-111; **Sperry Top-Sider**, 6-11, 12, 13, 14; **Sportif**, 4-18; **U.S. Cavalry Store**, 6-39; **Utica Duxbak**, 5-8, 9, 10; **White's Shoes**, 6-74, 75, 76; **E.T. Wright**, 6-16, 17.

Contents

ACKNOWLEDGMENTS

We would like to express our deepest admiration and thanks to Mr. John J. Anderson, former Director of the U.S. Navy Clothing Research and Development Lab, who generously donated his expertise and many hours to this book and whose help has been invaluable. And to Mr. Seymour Lash, Director of Clothing Development, our host at Natick who devoted an entire day to answering questions and putting his expert staff at our disposal.

We would also like to offer special thanks to the members of the J.C. Penney Clothing Evaluation and Testing Division, in particular Mssrs. James Stavrakas, Martin Gavlak, and Aubrey Jay. They graciously shared their extensive knowledge with us and provided indispensible assistance in the research for this book. Throughout, we were consistently impressed by their honesty and dedication to quality control.

Our deepest gratitude to Don Davies, Al Denigris, Don Huxley, Walter Schaefer, Dr. James Veghte, and Dr. Dorothy Lyle.

Our sincerest thanks, also, to the Pentax Corporation for their generous loan of camera equipment.

Introduction

People complain, and for the most part they're right, that it is hard to find good quality clothes these days: "They just don't make them like they used to." Across the country, there is a growing disenchantment with seductively promoted consumer goods. People are beginning to see popular fashion wear for what it often is—contrived, overpriced, and planned for obsolescence, irrelevant to the direction of our lives and the times—and to seek out practical clothing that will last.

There is something undeniably pleasing and fulfilling about being able to continue wearing some dependable garment or pair of shoes for many years after its purchase. They become reliable friends. And like friends, you must care for them as they care for you. These are not fashion clothes to be cast off for rags after just a season or two.

We are fortunate enough to have clothes that we have been collecting gradually over a period of years. We have tweed jackets that are 10 years old and look as appropriate and stylish now as the day they were bought. We've got boots that tell a similar story. These clothes have lived with us as we have with them. Their vigorous life may be drawing to a close but meanwhile, new members of the collection are being very selectively added.

In the course of our search for these enduring clothes, we came to wonder why a source guide had never been written on the subject. A book that would explain not only where to find these clothes and the elemental shopping techniques for recognizing quality clothing, but also how your body and your clothes work together, how you can best use your clothes, and how to care for them.

The various clothing and footwear presented here are distinguished examples of practical clothing available in America today. These clothes offer a rational and constructive alternative to the tiresome and wasteful gimmickry of conventional fashion. The emphasis here is on utility, durability, effectiveness of design, ease of maintenance, and timeless styling. It is an eclectic gathering, culled from predominantly outdoor occupations and pursuits—from forestry to aviation. Here, function and efficiency have traditionally received priority.

The first serious study of clothing for function rather than appearance was undertaken by the U.S. government during World War II. When Pearl Harbor was attacked in 1941, our Armed Forces were outfitted with snappy dress uniforms but their field gear was woefully inadequate. As one observer put it, we were equipped to fight in Maine in the summer and Florida in the winter. Fortunately for us all, the Germans belatedly discovered the same truth during their disastrous winter Eastern offensive, when lack of proper clothing is said to have caused them twice as many casualties as the Russians' bullets.

Few people may realize or appreciate the extremely detailed and intensive research the government conducts on clothing and footwear. The principal center for this work is at the Army and Navy Natick Laboratories in Massachusetts. These facilities are known and respected all over the world for having one of the foremost clothing research and development programs. Although most of this research is initially for military applications, a great part of it eventually contributes to improving civilian clothing.

In terms of practicality, members of the American Armed Forces have been among the best-dressed people in our society. And standing in the Navy labs, far from the hoopla of Seventh Avenue, we saw what results are possible in clothing when intelligent reasoning and integrity prevail.

The fashion industry, on the other hand, is geared to constant change, is in fact founded upon "psychological obsolescence," like so many of our consumer goods. It can be a tremendously profitable business, but one that also involves a high degreee of gambling. And because of this, manufacturers have to hedge their bets.

Fashion manufacturers typically put out several seasonal lines a year. Because fashion is so fickle, they make up each line as close to its selling time as possible, and as a result, they have to pay premium prices for rush orders on fabric and labor. In the rush, they often have scant time to pay close attention to details of workmanship.

Indeed, the fashion companies seldom make their own garments; they contract them out. And contractors also try to cut corners by skimping on seams and hems and perhaps even cutting each garment a little small. This way, they save enough yardage to either sell the extra fabric or to make up garments to sell themselves. The company too looks for shortcuts in the garment make before sending the order to the contractor: ways to leave out a lining, for example, or cut back on some of the construction to save labor costs. This results in a shoddy garment with the same high price tag.

And because fashion companies know there is a good chance that a fashion may not be accepted by the public, they have to add enough cushioning to their already inflated price to cover their losses if a fashion is a bust-out. Similarly, the retailer, as insurance, typically *at least* doubles the already inflated price.

In order to further reduce the risk and maximize the profit, each season fashion companies and retailers spend vast sums of money in advertising and promotions to sell the public on their fashions. And don't be fooled; you pay for all this advertising and promotional gimmickry as well as for the garment itself—it's all figured into the price tag.

Designer labels have come to play a big part in this promotional gimmickry. Big-name designers rarely see the products being sold under their names, let alone actually design them or exercise any quality control over them. They simply make a deal to lease their names, for a hefty royalty, to the makers of neckties or sweaters or what have you, knowing that many people are seduced by famous fashion names and will pay richly to have them. You can easily pay 75 percent, 100 percent, and even higher for a "designer" garment that doesn't offer anything more than a trendy label and the designer's initials. Frequently, the identical garment is being sold at the same time under another label for a considerably lower price.

Designer labels are not the only ones for which you pay extra. Certain stamps of approval such as the Olympic Games medallions, designating the manufacturer as an official supplier to the Olympics, can be purchased by a manufacturer at a considerable expense and, again, that cost is passed on to you.

In all fairness, it's to some degree the customer's responsibility that value in clothing continues to decline. You vote each time you buy. If you're undiscriminating and passively accept whatever is offered you without complaint, then the retailer is far less likely to demand a better product from the clothing company. And if the clothing company does not get pressure from the retailer, it's unlikely the company will attempt to improve its product. No businessperson is going to offer a better product when there appears to be no demand for it.

We would like to stress that all of the companies selected for mention in this book were chosen by us on a strictly private and independent basis, completely free from any kind of remuneration or inducements, financial or otherwise.

We have made a sincere and committed effort to select only the best examples of practical clothing. It is important to appreciate that they represent a sampling only of what is currently available and, excellent as they are, there remains ample room for improvements and diversity.

CLOTHING:

PART ONE

OUR SECOND SKIN

1

Environmental Dressing

"Our clothes are too much a part of us for most of us ever to be entirely indifferent to their condition; it is as though the fabric were indeed a natural extension of the body, or even of the soul."

Quentin Bell, *On Human Finery*

When you stop to think about it, you are almost always dressing for a temperate climate, whatever the time of year. Because so many people consider spring and fall weather conditions to be pretty much ideal, our homes and offices are maintained at this climate year round.

Dr. Paul Siple of the U.S. Army and renowned expert in clothing research observes: "[In a temperate climate] the body so completely adjusts itself . . . that it is well able to adapt itself even to mistakes in clothing design. As a consequence, people living in these [temperate] zones for all or part of the year tend to emphasize fashion which may entail considerable variation in quantity and style from year to year. . . . In practice, clothing in this zone is inclined more often to be ornamental or fashionable than to follow any sound scientific principle." Given the present economic and energy crunch, however, there is a lot less room now for such mistakes or extravagances in the clothes we buy.

Living in a temperate indoor climate, there is even less need than you might realize for separate wardrobes for summer, winter, spring, and fall. Clothing for spring and fall, if selected with forethought, can comfortably serve into the winter as well. Simply add additional layers to punch up the warmth. For the depths of summer heat though, you may indeed require a back-up selection of especially cool, lightweight clothing. But even lightweight summer pants and shirts, and so on, can, if desired, be worn throughout the spring and fall and often even into the winter. It is only color and style that typecast your clothes to a very limited time of year.

This gives you the most versatile basic wardrobe you can have. When the temperature is warm, you can wear just a single layer of your clothing. And when it gets cool, adding several layers—for example, wearing an undershirt, shirt, and light sweater—will keep you warmer than wearing a heavy sweater alone. A few thin layers are al-ways significantly warmer than a single layer of equal thickness because the air spaces between each layer provide additional insulation.

Also, if you can wear your same basic clothing year round, stripping down in the summer and layering up in the winter (instead of feeling obligated to invest in several separate wardrobes), then you may be able to afford to buy a few more year-round clothes of better quality. And if you have a few more clothes, then each will receive less use in a given year and will therefore probably last that much longer.

Dressing yourself in a practical way is the art of buying selectively, the art of discriminating between what you need and can use from what you want just for the sake of having it. A lot of people buy clothing impulsively, as if from nervous habit.

Fashion proponents have frequently raised the objection to us: "Well, people become bored with wearing the same clothing after a while so why invest in good, long-lasting clothes?" This objection may be valid but to a large degree it is the fashion industry that has worked diligently to condition us to quickly tire of our clothes and also to doubt our own ability to make long-term decisions for ourselves.

If you do tire of something, stick it in the back of your closet and give it a rest. Chances are that you will rediscover your appreciation for it after a while.

LIVING IN WARDROBE

The moment you put on a stitch of clothing, it becomes an integral part of your body's thermal workings. If you want to take a sensible and more practical approach to wearing clothes, then it's important to have some insight into the ways your body and your clothing work together. The purpose of this section is to provide a basic understanding of how your body's mechanisms of thermal regulation (in other words, why you feel cold and why you feel hot) are influenced by clothes.

Like all mammals and also birds, we are warm-blooded beings, which means we maintain a constant internally regulated body temperature, as opposed to cold-blooded creatures (whose body temperature is determined by the external environment) such as insects, reptiles, and certain varieties of landlords.

Your body is continuously generating heat, produced by your 100 trillion or so cells. Some of this nonstop heat production must be unloaded in order to maintain the constant or "steady-state" body temperature. Heat production must be balanced by a proportionate amount of heat loss. Your skin plays a crucial role in this process.

In the complex and everchanging world of modern technological society, skin is still one of humanity's best allies. It is by far the largest of the human organs: it covers over 20 square feet of surface area on the average adult; weighs in at about 6 pounds; and receives about one-third of all blood circulating through the body.

In response to the environment, skin temperature is largely governed by vasodilation and vasoconstriction, which means the expansion and contraction of cutaneous (skin) blood vessels. In a hot environment, these cutaneous vessels expand, thus permitting more blood to flow to the skin surface and release heat. When the environment is cold, the blood vessels contract, reducing blood flow to the skin, and thereby conserving heat. "Thermostats" deep within the nerve centers of the brain act as the master control for this intricate regulation of internal heat balance.

From the skin's surface, heat is then physically released by means of conduction, convection, evaporation, or radiation and any combination of these four.

Conduction comes into play when your body touches something cooler or hotter than itself. Obviously, under normal conditions, this is a very minor way to either gain or lose heat. But if, for example, you get your feet wet, water is an excellent conductor and wet socks and shoes will conduct your body heat away from you into the colder ground.

Convective heat loss is continually occurring as air movement around you absorbs your heat and carries it away. Because the surrounding air temperature is commonly cooler than your skin, you usually lose heat by convection, but if the air is hotter, you will gain heat by convection.

Forced convective heat loss occurs when the movement of air around you is rapidly accelerated, as by the wind or an electric fan, for example. Blown air transports your body heat away at a much faster rate.

The windchill factor is a measurement for expressing the increased cooling effect (forced convective heat loss) produced by a given wind speed. For instance, at 40° F, a 10 mph wind creates a windchill of 28° F, which means that on a 40° F day, a 10 mph wind will so accelerate your body's (or any object's warmer than 40° F) rate of heat loss as to simulate the effect of a windless 28° F day.

That does not mean that a puddle of water under such conditions would freeze as if it were in fact 28° F outdoors, because the actual ambient temperature, regardless of windchill, still remains at 40° F. All that happens is that the puddle will cool more rapidly to 40° F than it would if there were no wind and, in fact, will cool to 40° F as rapidly as if it were 28° F out. Windchill, however, cannot cool an object below the real ambient temperature.

Radiation put in simplified terms is heat energy emitted as particles or waves. Heat is actually part of the electromagnetic spectrum, which means that you can think of radiant heat as behaving like visible light or even more like radio signals. Your whole body acts as a radio transmitter continuously sending out heat in very much the same way that a transmitter broadcasts radio signals.

Radiation is an important avenue of heat loss because you are frequently surrounded by objects that are cooler than your skin temperature. So, therefore, your body is continually emitting heat to its surrounding cooler environment. Radiative heat loss is much less from skin areas that are close together, such as the fingers and toes, and the thighs and underarms. Similarly, when two or more people are huddled together, radiative (and also convective) heat loss is reduced.

Evaporation cools you because liquids require heat in order to evaporate. Night and day, your skin is continually being lightly moistened by "insensible perspiration" which is the imperceptible constant supply of moisture your body provides the skin. This moisture absorbs your body heat as it evaporates, carrying the heat away with it. So even when you're just sitting around in a comfortable temperature, about one-third of your body's heat production is being carried off by the perpetual evaporation of insensible perspiration.

Evaporative cooling greatly increases when you start to sweat, whether from heat, exertion, or emotion. The purpose of sweating is to cool the overheated body by a marked increase in evaporation. If the relative humidity is high (specifically, over 80 percent), however, then evaporation becomes impeded and sweat beads up on your skin, making you feel sticky and clammy.

In a temperate environment, when you are not being particularly active, these four avenues of heat loss successfully counterbalance your body's heat production.

But, as the temperature gets colder, and if you remain inactive, you lose a lot more heat by radiation and by convection. Proper clothing becomes essential to protect you against an excessive loss of heat. On the other hand, when the temperature rises and approaches that of your skin temperature, you lose very little heat by radiation and convection because your body is no longer warmer than its surrounding environment. So you have to start sweating to lose more heat. When the temperature reaches about 95° F, evaporation becomes the only way you can lose heat. If the mercury continues to climb, you actually absorb heat from the environment.

WEARING AIR

Like it or not, when you cover yourself with clothing, you are insulating your body, however slightly. Any fabric, no matter how gossamer, has some insulative value and will impede the release of heat and moisture. Even the sheerest nylon stockings provide some insulation against the cold and make you noticeably hotter in the summer.

But contrary to what you might think, it is not the actual fabric that keeps you warm; it is in fact the *air* trapped within the fabric. The warmth of a fabric is determined by how much air it contains. No one textile material is, to any significant degree, intrinsically warmer than any other; warmth depends on fabric *thickness* because the thicker the fabric, the greater its volume of air. The greater the volume of air, the more insulating power the fabric has.

So, contrary to popular folk wisdom, the old notion that if a winter garment is heavy, it must be warm, is utterly incorrect. If it was indeed warm, the only reason was because it was thick. Weight has no bearing on warmth, but air does.

Air is such an excellent body insulator because it is a very poor conductor of heat. It is also very lightweight and extremely flexible. The one slight problem with air is that it circulates. If the air is allowed to circulate freely, then you lose heat by convection. The air next to your body absorbs heat; this warmed air then expands and rises and is immediately replaced by cooler air, which in turn is warmed and rises and is replaced, and so on. This heat loss cycle will continue as long as there is still heat to be lost (more specifically, until the temperatures on either side of the insulation are the same—like when you're dead). In addition, convective heat loss is accelerated by wind and by the constant bellowslike pumping action created inside your clothing when you move around.

Consequently, in order to make use of air as a truly effective insulator, it must be restricted or immobilized as much as possible. So what a fabric does is simply contain, confine, and immobilize this air. The extent to which a garment can maintain a layer of immobilized or so-called "dead air" around you determines its worth as an insulator. Oddly enough, the ideal insulator would be a vacuum and if you can think of a way to design an overcoat that works like a Thermos bottle, is practical for daily wear, and is also affordable, the world will beat a path to your door.

The relation of thickness to insulative power, for all intents and purposes, applies to all clothing textiles and any one of them is as warm as the next. So don't let anyone try to tell you that wool is effectively warmer than cotton or that one wool is warmer than another wool. Always remember, for all practical purposes, *thickness determines warmth.*

WINTER TACTICS

Dressing to keep warm in winter is decidedly easier than dressing to remain comfortable in torrid summer heat. If this doesn't conform with your experience, then you owe it to yourself to reconsider your methods of winter dress. After all, "cold" refers only to the relative absence of heat. It is not, as some people seem to feel, some kind of preternatural force that hides in alleys and sneaks up on you in the middle of the night. Believe us, once you have learned the basic techniques for staying warm and comfortable, winter takes on a wonderful new appeal.

The feeling of cold is simply the sensation of your skin temperature dropping; it's the loss of heat to the environment at a faster rate than you are able to produce it. If you can properly protect against this heat loss, then you won't feel cold. This is quite possible to do. Cold is always a relative term: someone engaged in strenuous activity whose body is generating a great deal of heat will naturally feel warmer than a sedentary person in the same environment whose metabolism (basically, the production of heat by the body) is functioning at a lower rate.

Similarly, many of you have probably experienced in the summer how, if the temperature suddenly drops to 60° F, you feel cold and rush to put on a sweater. Yet in the middle of winter, if a sudden warm spell occurs and the temperature rises to the same 60° F, you say "What a beautiful day" and walk around in your shirt sleeves.

There is no such thing as cold gain; you can only have heat loss. Clothing, in and of itself, is not warm; *you* are what is warm. All clothing can do is provide insulation to impede heat from escaping from your body.

So you want to create a zone or layer around your body that effectively impedes heat loss. This doesn't necessarily mean you want to shut off all heat loss completely; in such a case, the temperature inside your clothing would rise to very uncomfortable levels. You just want to be able to control heat loss in order to maintain a comfortable, reasonably constant, skin temperature.

The two basic ways to accomplish this are to insulate and to seal up any place where warm air could escape and cold air could invade. As we've said before, as far as common clothing insulation is concerned: THICKNESS = WARMTH, and warmth does not necessarily mean weight. In fact, the minimizing of weight is always a desirable aim in terms of comfort because you will feel less restricted, less inhibited by your clothing. After all, what good is it to be warm if you have to trundle down the street like an overwrapped mummy?

This is the great advantage of down and fiberfills, which provide a high degree of insulation with a minimum amount of weight. In fact, it's sometimes hard to understand why down and fiberfill outerwear has not become the absolute preferred mode of winter attire. We both remember how, when we first experienced wearing down, we had to remind ourselves occasionally that we weren't cold. We were so used to being miserable and hating winter that it took our minds a little while to register the fact that we were warm despite the icy wind blowing on our faces. Once you've experienced down's remarkable comfort and freedom from restrictive weight and bulk, it becomes hard to even consider wearing any other kind of cold-weather coat.

You also want to seal those points where warm air can escape and cold air can penetrate. Principal points are collar, cuffs, and waist: your coat collar should be insulated and fit snugly around your neck (a scarf and/or turtleneck will help here); your cuffs should have either knitted wristlets or a closure so they too can be snugged around your wrists; and an inside drawcord around your waist will also seal in warmth. These same principles apply to your inner clothing as well.

Layering is a very good general principle for dressing. It allows you greater flexibility in your wardrobe because you can simply add a layer or two to your year-round clothing rather than buy separate complete wardrobes for summer and winter. Also, with layers of clothing, you can regulate your temperature more easily by opening or removing layers as comfort requires.

Keeping your torso well-insulated has been found to be far more effective in conserving heat and maintaining your sense of comfort than insulation anywhere else. Any additional layer of clothing over your torso will noticeably increase your insulation and feeling of comfort. The addition of a down, fiberfill, or even wool vest can make the difference between being comfortable and having the shivers.

In fact, there can be as much as a 20° F difference in temperature between your torso and your feet without this being any cause for concern or even for a feeling of discomfort. Indeed, cool hands and feet can be an advantage because this acts as a signal for the body to conserve heat. The flow of blood to the skin and to the extremities will be strategically diminished in order to reduce additional heat loss and to concentrate body heat in the most crucial regions, specifically the torso and the brain.

It is a well-established physiological fact that, in cold weather, it is preferable for your hands and feet to be somewhat cooler than your torso; you will feel more comfortable if this is the case. Experiments have shown that when the hands and feet are overinsulated to such a degree as to guarantee their warmth, the rest of the body, even though well-clothed, is cold and shivery; but when the same test subjects are dressed so their hands and feet are slightly cool, they feel comfortably warm in spite of their cooler extremities. Apparently, "overdressing" the hands and feet tricks the body into not recognizing the need to conserve heat and therefore you become chilled. You can

always rub your hands together and stamp your feet to warm them but if your whole body is shivering, no matter how warm your feet are, you will feel awful. Incidentally, it has also been found that having slightly cool hands and feet keeps you more alert.

Obviously, this doesn't mean you should leave your hands and feet unprotected, or that allowing your extremities to get cold, rather than just cool, is going to make the rest of you any warmer.

Wearing mittens is much warmer than wearing gloves because hands shrouded in mittens provide significantly less surface area for heat loss. You can wear a pair of thin gloves, even fingerless gloves, inside so that when you want to handle something, you can just slip off your mittens and your hands will still be protected.

A common adage among outdoor people is that wearing a hat will keep your feet warm. There is a lot of truth in this; wearing a hat will help conserve overall body heat and thus may well prevent your feet from getting uncomfortably cold (although once your feet have gotten cold, putting on a hat won't warm them up again). As mentioned earlier, the blood flow to the head (specifically for the brain) remains fairly constant regardless of temperature. Consequently, your head acts like a big radiator. Just to make matters worse, the spherical shape of the head happens to be an excellent configuration for heat loss because a sphere offers maximum surface area in proportion to volume. Heat loss from the unprotected head is substantial: at 60° F, you lose one-third of all your body heat from the head; at 5° F, three-quarters is lost. Even a modest protection for the scalp will preserve much of this heat.

Sensations of chill or discomfort to your head are a poor guide as to whether you need a hat because your body's internal thermostat naturally maintains head temperature at a constant fixed level of warmth. Unlike the arms and legs, where blood flow may be considerably reduced to conserve heat for the rest of the body, blood flow to the head will actually increase, if necessary, in order to maintain the head's warmth. Not surprisingly, if cooled blood from your head keeps circulating back to the torso, it will soon cause a drop in your overall body temperature.

KEEPING YOUR INSULATION DRY

It is most important not to let your insulation get wet, whether by perspiration or by rain or snow, because this drastically reduces its effectiveness. When insulation gets wet, the insulating air spaces become filled with moisture. Water, unlike air, is an excellent conductor of heat and will readily conduct your body heat right through your clothing to the outside. There will also be an additional heat loss through evaporation when this moisture absorbs your body heat.

Over the last few years, especially in backpacking circles, there has been a wave of enthusiastic advocacy of wool as the outdoorsman's wonder fiber. Most of this is just a lot of cracker-barrel folklore. There's no doubt that wool is a marvelous material. Nevertheless, contrary to modern folk mythology, wool is not significantly water-repellent and it will become saturated in the rain. Like any other fiber, wool does not retain its insulating properties when it becomes saturated.

There is one other myth about wool that is particularly ludicrous. It is a scientific fact that a small quantity of heat is released when wool absorbs water. As far as human comfort is concerned, however, the amount of heat released is hardly enough to warm a sickly caterpillar. So don't let anyone pull the wool over your eyes by proclaiming that wet wool somehow generates warmth.

It is crucial to keep your clothing dry by ventilating against undue perspiring and by protecting it from rain and snow. A light outer shell garment of a tightly woven fabric which fits comfortably over your down or fiberfill coat without compressing the loft will protect you from short exposures to precipitation. It will also provide a significant degree of added insulation on a windy or particularly cold day. The windchill factor can make a tolerable 30° F temperature feel like 10° F with just the help of a breezy 15 mph wind. Wind penetrates your clothing, rapidly accelerating convective heat loss and thereby cutting the insulative value by as much as 50 percent. A tightly woven, even though thin, overgarment can greatly cut down on this wind penetration and windchill heat loss.

Although a mountain shell will protect you against light rain, wind, and even increase your warmth, it cannot protect you from heavy rain. For this, you will need a truly waterproof, as opposed to water-repellent, outer shell.

Unfortunately, no totally satisfactory material has yet been found that combines waterproofness with air permeability. If the material is coated so no water can penetrate from the outside, then moisture vapor from your body may condense so heavily on the inside that it will wet your insulation, thereby reducing its effectiveness. If the material is permeable enough to prevent condensation of body moisture on the inside, rain eventually can seep in.

DOG-DAY MEASURES

Summertime, and the living is easy—supposedly. But if you're not water-skiing, on vacation in northern Canada, or in a nice, air-conditioned bar, summer heat and humidity can be sheer torture. The heat your body is producing has no place to go.

Your internal temperature regulation does the best it can: extra blood flow is shunted to the skin, the cutaneous blood vessels expand, sweating increases. But although the system is generally good enough to prevent injury to your health, it can't do much to improve your feelings of comfort. And clothes, no matter how little you wear, additionally interfere with heat elimination.

The ideal, of course, would be to not wear any clothes at all but unfortunately this is seldom a legal option. So you have to settle for making yourself as comfortable as you can.

When your skin is hot and sticky, it is in a very sensitized condition and more susceptible to irritation. One of the best ways to maximize your comfort, short of hanging out in a meat locker, is to wear smooth, silky fabrics that feel good against your skin. Such fabrics cause the least irritation and will feel soothing. Obvious as this may sound, it does work, and for sound, scientific reasons.

Fabrics are largely made up of air, which is insulative. The higher the percentage of actual conductive fiber, as opposed to nonconductive air, and the greater the contact of the fabric with your skin, the cooler it will feel. Smooth, woven fabrics, such as a thin, long staple cotton, will feel cooler to the touch than a hairy, less dense material such as wool. This is because, when you touch something cooler than yourself, your skin is registering the rate of heat loss or, in other words, the flow of heat away from your body to the object. Ironing a garment smoothes out the fabric surface even further which increases its overall contact with the skin and makes it feel cooler than a wrinkled garment.

Wherever possible, you want to be sure the clothing you have to wear will provide the absolute minimum of insulation. Fabrics, in addition to being smooth-surfaced, should be thin and of open or loose weave, to maximize ventilation. Because your arms and legs make up a large percentage of your total body surface area, they are a very important means of losing heat and should remain uncovered whenever possible. Anything that traps heat inside your clothing should be abolished. This includes tight collars; most definitely ties, which not only close off ventilation around the neck but add additional insulating layers of fabric; snugly fitting cuffs; and anything that restricts your waist.

In summer, loose fitting garments are always more comfortable because they maximize ventilation and circulation of air through your clothes. Every time you move, especially in loose clothing, you create a "bellows" action which pumps air through your clothing, thereby producing additional cooling. So leaving your shirt untucked will make you feel a lot cooler. In addition, if your clothes are damp from sweat, loose garments are less likely to cling to you, feeling sticky, clammy, and uncomfortable. Jeans in hot weather are just plain lunacy. Their dense weave and the snug, body-fitting cut will cook you alive.

Suspenders are frequently cooler than a belt because your trousers are not cinched in at the waist, cutting off air circulation. Suspenders, however, do press down on your shoulders and back, so wear ones that are as narrow as possible in hot weather.

No matter what you do, your feet will be hot and sweaty. Feet and hands have a much higher number of sweat glands than any other part of your body. Your best bet for comfort is sandals with no socks. A regular shoe encases your foot in a leather package and, although leather does "breathe" to a limited extent, it's not enough to offset the fact that the shoe is insulating your foot. Nothing short of installing a mini-air conditioner in your shoes will keep the temperature cool down there. Wear as thin a sock as possible. Here, tactile comfort is more important than the material of the sock; we personally prefer a smooth, silky sock.

Remember that loose clothing can offer some important shade protection against the sun's radiant heat. As far as color goes, contrary to common folk wisdom, light-colored clothing is not substantially cooler than black clothing. Based on the results of desert research supplied to us by the U.S. Air Force, the color of clothing for all practical purposes is of no great importance in reducing summer heat discomfort, even under blazing sun.

The question of durability is particularly important in summer clothing. Because you want the fabric to be thin, it may also tend to be somewhat weak unless of very high quality. Many man-made fibers are far stronger than natural fibers, so a blend is an advantage in terms of durability, though some people claim that man-mades are "hotter" or "less comfortable" than natural fibers. There is, as of yet, no conclusive scientific evidence to show this one way or the other; so it remains a matter of personal preference.

One last note: Because the body is an integral unit, cooling in one area will cool off the entire system. So if you can, for example, hold your wrists under the cold tap for a few minutes, this will cool you down a little all over and provide some relief, at least temporarily.

GOOD GARB

PART TWO

SOURCE GUIDE

Mail-Order Shopping

"Taste is a matter of choice
but quality is a matter of fact."

—Andre Simon

To a large extent, high-quality functional clothing exists in a realm off the beaten trail. For the most part, you just can't walk into a department store or a shopping mall and start buying the kinds of clothes presented in this book. Small specialty shops here and there may carry some items but the main source presently is mail-order catalogs.

Some people are leery about mail-order shopping. But, at least with respect to the quality mail-order sources compiled herein, there is no question in our minds that they are in many ways superior to most local merchants, in terms of quality merchandise, customer service, and guarantees.

Like your local retailer, catalog houses have a name and a reputation to maintain. Unlike the local merchant, they get no off-the-street traffic and must rely heavily on satisfied customers for return business and to spread their reputation.

Consequently, they must positively ensure that the quality of their goods and services at least meets with or even exceeds their customers' standards. In no way can they afford to monkey around with low-grade, substandard merchandise. Often, many of the items featured in a given catalog will reappear season after season, serving testimony to their time-proven success and reliability.

This doesn't mean that a lemon won't turn up occasionally. Most catalog houses, however, have firm "satisfaction guaranteed or your money back" policies and they do stand behind them. You'll see in the listing in the back that several offer unconditional lifetime guarantees. We once had to return a garment that proved faulty three years after its purchase, and our money and postage were promptly refunded with no questions asked. So it's very much in the catalog houses' interests to run a tight ship because shoddy merchandise could easily mean a loss for them of thousands of dollars of profits in returns, lost customers, and bad publicity.

To some people, many of the prices quoted here may seem high. The real question, however, is not so much price by itself as *value,* value being the ability of a product to provide the greatest and widest amount of useful service in proportion to dollars invested. In this respect, the clothing assembled here constitutes distinctly economical investments.

Prices listed are as of September 1980; they should be understood as being *close approximations.*

Because we've all been so conditioned by advertising and convention to think in terms of shopping for clothes in stores, the notion of mail-order shopping may, if you haven't tried it, at first seem alien. We know a lot of people worry about size, fit, and color, and how such a selection can be made from a picture. This has never caused us any problem.

Mail-order shopping is a minor exercise in delayed gratification. Remember that finding the correct size, fit, and color in a department store is usually no picnic anyway. Gauging your size correctly from a catalog entails an element of uncertainty that can't be avoided, but if something is not quite right when you get it, just mail it back for a full refund or an exchange if you prefer. We like to hedge our bets by ordering two sizes in a particular garment, which allows us the convenience of comparing which of the two fits better. Then just return the reject.

Based on our experience and from the experiences of many of our friends, we're convinced that shopping *quality* mail-order companies is one of the best, most convenient, and dependable ways to assemble a quality wardrobe.

Zeroing In on Quality: General Guidelines

With the current popularity of what some are calling "outdoor chic," many designers and manufacturers are producing clothes to *look* functional. And that's as far as the function goes. Design, materials, and workmanship have not been considered with real use or durability in mind; only the appearance has been given attention.

When you are looking for the genuine article, just a little knowledge and thought will enable you to distinguish between the two. That doesn't mean that you have to educate yourself extensively on what goes into the making of a garment. After all, there may be roughly 200 steps involved in making a quality shirt; as many or more in making a good pair of shoes. Many of these steps cannot ever be seen in the finished product, even though they constitute an essential part of its makeup.

However, you can learn to judge the intelligence of a design; you can glean something about the quality of the materials; and you can also get a good reading on the overall workmanship by examining the finish work.

There are two main areas to examine: the *make,* which includes both the quality of construction and of the fabric and findings like snaps and zippers; and the *design,* in terms of its practicality, whether it works for you and whether it fits you properly.

THE MAKE

To check the fabric quality, hold the material up to the light. In general, the closer and more even the weave or knit, the stronger the fabric. It is also more wind resistant. At this stage in history, however, it is not yet feasible to mass-produce perfectly uniform fabric. Even the finest fabrics will reveal, upon close inspection, some degree of irregularity. But if you start to make a practice of comparing fabrics, you will quickly develop a feel for gauging when the degree of inconsistency is substandard.

For thin knits in particular, one will sometimes see areas where the yarn has been spun or knit very unevenly, resulting in thin patches. Not only is this a sign of poor quality control, which suggests that other aspects of the garment may be equally shoddy, but also these thin areas are weak and will wear out sooner.

A hard, smooth finish will generally show fewer signs of wear and be more durable than a fluffier textured surface. Bulky fabrics are warmer, however.

If possible, clip a yarn from a raw edge of the fabric. Untwist it to see how many strands it has: two- or more ply yarn is sturdier than single ply (see p. 169).

If the fabric is napped, be sure the nap on all pieces faces in the same direction. The nap on outdoor clothes and pants should face down to shed rain and dirt. Where such considerations are less important, nap that faces upward will look richer and more lush.

Bonded or laminated fabrics, where the fabric and its lining or interlining are fused together as one, can mean real trouble; they may bubble, pucker, and separate. Dry cleaning and steam pressing can also cause these problems. There is no way that you can judge in advance whether or not the laminate will hold—you can only rely on the integrity of the retailer. If you do have such problems, by all means return the garment without hesitation.

Check the garment label for fabric content. Virgin wool is generally preferable to reprocessed; long staple cottons and wools make finer, stronger yarns than short staple fibers; blends of three or more fibers may mean that the fabric is made from the floor sweepings of the mill. Some triblends, however, are legitimate. On the whole, a fabric must contain at least 15 to 20 percent of any given fiber for that fiber to make any worthwhile contribution to the fabric's performance, *except* in the case of such fibers as spandex or rubber.

Fabric grain should run straight in the garment. Vertical threads in sleeves should fall straight from shoulder to cuff; horizontal threads should run straight across. Otherwise, the garment will not hang well and is likely to twist and distort in washing. Fabrics cut on the bias and twill weaves are exceptions, of course.

Color should be even, without streaks. Better quality patterned fabrics are yarn-dyed, with the colors clearly visible on the reverse side. Pigment printed patterns, where the color is essentially "painted" on the surface, tend to wear off. Here again, there is no conclusive way of determining on the spot whether or not a color or pattern will hold up. The integrity of the retailer is your only guide. Plaids, stripes, and diagonal lines should match nicely along seams.

All parts of a garment must be compatible. If the main fabric is washable, then the interfacings, linings, trim, and so forth must also be washable and must shrink to the same degree; this they don't tell you on the label. Equally, if the garment fabric is "preshrunk," the thread used must be also or needless puckering and poor fit will result. If such problems do develop, return the garment.

Fabrics that are resin-treated to provide wash and wear or other special characteristics tend to be weakened by these finishes. Also, some resins will absorb chlorine and tend to yellow; fabrics that are chemically modified maintain their appearance more satisfactorily.

One of the most telling signs about a garment is the finish work. After all, all garments, from the worst to the best, consist of just a few simple seams. The cost of the material itself, with a few exceptions, is relatively small. The main cost and the part that is most time-consuming is the finish work. How well are the buttonholes made and the buttons sewn on; is the stitching small, neat, and even, with no skipped stitches and no puckering of the fabric; are the seam edges cleanly finished; have stress points been reinforced with bar tacks of good quality? Check the garment thoroughly both inside and out.

THE DESIGN

If the garment meets with your approval so far, then the next thing to consider is fit. Does it fit properly? Fit is completely separate from the size. If the fit is not right for your body shape, no size will work. Does the garment hang well? Look for unsightly pulls or wrinkles. Does it bind anywhere? Armholes and the pants crotch should not be cut so deep that they actually constrict your movement. Is there enough material through the legs and seat, across your back, not to put strain on the seams when you're active?

It is a well-established fact that a properly fitted garment will actually last longer and not wear out as quickly as an ill-fitting one. In those cases where you fall between sizes, however, in our opinion it's preferable, from a wear standpoint, to go with the slightly larger size as long as it's not too large.

Consider the design for ease of movement and convenience of use. Are the pockets at a comfortable angle for your hands and will what you put in them stay in? Are there enough pockets? Women's clothes in particular tend to skimp on such necessities.

The upshot of all this is: Will the garment perform the way you want it to, within realistic bounds? Will you feel comfortable in it, without its constricting or bothering you? Will you feel frustrated by evidence of poor workmanship or design? Or will you be pleased each time you wear it for a long time to come?

If the garment meets your standards, and you're pleased with the way it looks on you and will work for you, then buy it. If you're looking for quality and you're fortunate enough to find it, then you have to be prepared to pay for it. After all, if you wait too long, the price will only have gone up with inflation. On the whole, bargain hunting for these kinds of clothes is of questionable worth. Discount houses seldom prove fruitful. However, it always pays to keep your eyes peeled for a buy.

The price of the garment may seem high, but you're investing in something that will, with reasonable care, last you for a long, long time. If you consider the cost per wearing factor (divide the price of the garment by the number of times you expect to wear it), a $200 jacket that will last you at least 10 years will, if it doesn't just hang in your closet for a decade, prove to be a much more economical investment than some bargain basement cheapie.

If you are shopping for clothes that last, there is a certain minimum standard of quality below which it is simply not worth dropping. A poorly constructed garment made with cheap materials may have the general *look* of the real thing, but if you expect its performance to match its functional appearance, you will be sorely disappointed, even if you did pay less for it initially.

If a garment doesn't continue to meet with your satisfaction after purchase, then you should feel no compunctions about returning it. There is an implicit, legally binding guarantee that a product will perform according to its intended purpose. Manufacturers do make honest mistakes; if you don't inform the manufacturer, however, how can you expect him to correct it? It is unfair not to let him know you are dissatisfied and give him the chance to rectify the situation. In the case of just plain shoddy merchandise, by returning the garment, you inform the retailer and the manufacturer that this poor quality is unacceptable and that they cannot make money, at least from you, by continuing to sell it.

GARMENT LABELING

By law, certain informative labels are required on all apparel. When a garment is not being sold under a particular brand name, that is, is being sold "private label," it must then have a Registered Number (for example, RN6374) issued to the manufacturer by the Federal Bureau of Consumer Protection. This RN number, rather than the manufacturer's name, is used to identify the source of the item. You can call the Bureau of Consumer Protection in Washington, DC at (202) 724-1362 to find out who made the garment.

The Textile Fiber Products Identification Act went into effect in March 1960. Labels must be conspicuously attached. They must specify the generic name and the percentage of the fibers included; the name or RN number of the manufacturer; and, if the fabric is imported, the country of origin. Fibers or decorative trim that make up less than 5 percent of the garment are exempt. Linings, interlinings, fillings, and paddings must also be listed as to fiber content *only* if they are incorporated in the garment for warmth rather than for structural purposes. For example, the horsehair lining in a suit jacket need not be labeled because it is there purely for structural reasons, but the interlining of an overcoat would have to be identified. Stated fiber percentages may vary by 3 percent either more or less.

Wool products and fur products are each subject to separate labeling acts. All articles containing wool must be so labeled and the percentage thereof stated. If the wool is not virgin, the kind of wool used, whether reprocessed, reused, and so forth, must be specified. Specialty fibers, such as cashmere or angora, can be labeled as wool, but if they are named by their specialty name, the percentage used must be specified.

The Fur Products Labeling Act requires information on the English name of the animal from which the fur came; its country of origin; and whether the fur product is composed of used, damaged, or scrap fur, or fur that has been dyed or bleached.

The only garments required to be flame resistant are children's sleepwear and children's robes. The Flammable Fabrics Act requires that labels on apparel must clearly warn consumers if flame-retardant properties will be lessened or destroyed by home or commercial laundering.

The Federal Trade Commission's Permanent Care Labeling Rule went into effect in July 1972. The United States is the only country where it is mandatory by government regulation to label nearly all garments sold to consumers (including those imported from other countries) and to provide labels with yard goods sold to home sewers. The Rule requires "a label or tag permanently affixed or attached . . . to the finished article, which clearly discloses instructions for the care and maintenance of such article." The label must be easy to locate and must apply to all findings, such as buttons, zipper, and trim. Exempted items include those worn on the head, hands, and feet; and washable items selling for less than $3. Also, sheer or other items that would be substantially impaired by a label may be exempted by petition.

Proposed changes are now under consideration. Essentially these would clarify the Rule and expand it to include leather and suede apparel and household furnishings, and would establish a uniform reference for terms used in care instructions.

Under the current Rule, the label must disclose fully and clearly the regular care required; for example, how to wash, dry, iron, bleach, dry clean, and any other necessary procedures. It must also carry a warning if a usual care method appears to apply but in fact does not. For example, the FTC holds the position that the consumer takes for granted that if a garment is washable, then it is also dry-cleanable. Consequently, if this is not the case, it must be so labeled. White garments are considered bleachable according to fiber content; if a white garment cannot be bleached, the label must clearly indicate this. Because the FTC considers it a normal practice *not* to bleach colored fabrics, the manufacturer is not required to warn against this.

The FTC also takes the position that there are certain other care practices which are assumed to be common knowledge to consumers and therefore do not need to be stated on the label. These include: All fabrics are ironable under normal ironing conditions and all washable fabrics may also be dry cleaned unless the label specifies otherwise. The Rule avoids making specific requirements for care instructions, however, leaving these to the garment industries to develop.

Unfortunately, some labels can be confusing or of no help. One, seen by Dr. Dorothy Lyle while she was Director of Consumer Relations at the International Fabricare Institute, read as follows:

> **Sorry . . .**
> **Because of the widespread use of detergents and cleaning methods, and since we cannot control these methods of washing and cleaning, we cannot guarantee the washability or cleanability of any garment.**

If you run across one of these labels, we strongly recommend that you don't buy the garment—move on to another.

A fairly widespread, though illegal, practice is "low labeling." An example of this is labeling a washable garment "Dry Clean Only." There are several reasons for low labeling. One is that it allows the manufacturer not to test the garment for correct laundering procedures. Another is that, when a manufacturer is making up a line of garments, he can use the same label on all of them rather than having to print up separate labels for each item in his line.

However, before assuming the garment is washable even though it says "Dry Clean Only," you have to make sure that linings and all other parts of the garment can be washed and that all will shrink equally. Low labeling is a serious problem because it is very difficult for the consumer to judge when labeling is correct.

The International Fabricare Institute has established guidelines for the settlement of damage claims. The guidelines state that a textile article cleaned by an appropriate method is expected not to: shrink or stretch out of shape; become yellow, gray or otherwise discolored or changed physically in appearance; lose or change color, or stain other materials; become stiff, limp or otherwise changed in feel or touch.

Innerwear

SHIRTS

Here are the basic quality points to check for:

Front closure should have an interfacing for body and durability, whether placket type or French front. Check for well-made, closely overcast buttonholes of the correct size for the buttons; buttons should be sewn on firmly.

Placket front   **French front**

Cuff opening should have placket for neatness and durability. Cuff itself should be interfaced for reinforcement.

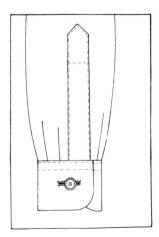

Cuff placket

Single-needle stitching, found most often on dress shirts, creates a strong, neat, flat seam with no raw edges. This better quality seam is more labor intensive because the maker has to run the seam through the sewing machine twice to create the two rows of stitching, whereas for a double-needle stitched seam, the double-needle machine accomplishes both stitchlines of the seam in a single run. Double-needle seams are much more likely to pucker.

A third, much cheaper alternative is the merrow- or serge-stitched seam, which, if done properly, can be quite strong but has a less finished appearance.

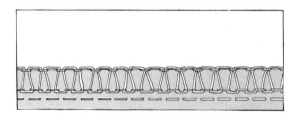

Serge stitch

Whatever type of seam is used, it is essential to have an adequate seam allowance or the seam will eventually rip out. This is especially true of man-made fabrics which tend to be slippery and are more subject to pulling out. Check for puckering along the seams. This is especially important on blends; puckered seams at the store mean puckered seams forever. This defect will not come out in the wash or with ironing; the stitch tension was incorrect when the seam was sewn.

The collar should align perfectly when the top button is closed; points should be neatly finished. A moderate shape collar style will endure indefinitely. Fused interlinings can bubble and separate; an interlining should simply be stitched into the seam to secure it. An extra patch of fabric under each collar point will keep them looking neat all day and also makes them more durable. Removable collar stays are preferable to ones that are permanently inserted. On a wool shirt, a satiny neck lining will be more comfortable against your neck.

Pockets should be bar tacked or backstitched. Look inside to be sure seam edges are cleanly finished; if left raw, they will soon start to fray. The pocket hem should be stitched down to prevent dirt collecting and small objects getting caught underneath. On patterned shirts, the pattern on the pockets should either match perfectly or be placed on a diagonal. Check for proper pattern matching at all points.

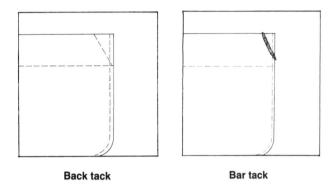

| Back tack | Bar tack |

Fabric in the back should be gathered evenly into the yoke. Tucks on either side of the shoulder blades provide more give. Tails should be of generous length to stay tucked in, an area that manufacturers often skimp on to save fabric. Check that shirt is neatly hemmed.

Any darts should come to a clean point, with no bubble, and should be positioned properly for you.

KNIT SHIRTS

On knit shirts, there are a few additional points to check. Hold the material up to the light to be sure the knit is reasonably uniform. Excessive thin areas not only are unattractive but are also weaker. Such lack of quality control at the yarn and knitting stage at least suggests an equal lack of quality care at other stages. Vertical lines in the knit are caused by dirt in the machines.

Examine all seams carefully to be sure there are no tiny holes (caused by the needle cutting the fabric as it sews); these can and probably will enlarge with wear. All raw edges must be serge-overlocked; check for this even in hidden areas such as the pocket hem. Be sure the seams stretch as much as the fabric does; if the fabric stretches more than the seam can, this is likely to cause the stitching to break.

Shoulder seams reinforced by seam tape will prevent them from distorting and stretching out excessively. Tape also reinforces this seam, which takes a lot of stress.

Fig.4-1

Fig.4-2

Fig.4-3

SHIRT SOURCES

Traditional Welsh flannel shirt in 100% pure wool flannel. Tough and hard-wearing, it is the standard pullover style, with a double thickness of flannel on the yoke. Material is cut as one continuous piece from front hem, over the shoulders, to the back hem. Yoke is a separate piece sewn on top. French seams contribute to the shirt's long life. Reinforcing gussets at cuff openings and side slits. Extra long back tail. Available from David Morgan. $45.*   **(Fig. 4-1)**

The Hickory shirt is worn by loggers in the Pacific Northwest. 100% tightly woven cotton. An unusual feature is the back, which is reinforced for 12″ down from the neck by a full-width second layer of fabric. An unusually durable shirt. Available from David Morgan. $14.   **(Fig. 4-2)**

Heavyweight pure wool shirt by Swanndri of New Zealand. Velour finish; specially treated for water repellency. Available from David Morgan. $41.   **(Fig. 4-3)**

*Prices listed are approximate and as of September 1980.

Fig.4-4

Fig.4-6

English sailor smocks are of heavy 100% cotton sailcloth. Available from David Morgan. $28.   **(Fig. 4-4)**

Welsh fisherman's smock of 100% wool flannel is full cut for free movement. Sleeves stop just short of the wrist, to keep them out of the fish. Two large pockets. Also shown is zipper front version. Available from David Morgan. $41. With zipper, $44.   **(Fig. 4-5)**

Welsh steelworker's vest is all wool flannel. Extra long backtail; loose cut sleeves. Sleeves and body seams are left unjoined for 2½" under arms to provide ventilation. Available from David Morgan. $40.   **(Fig. 4-6)**

Fig.4-5

Fig.4-7

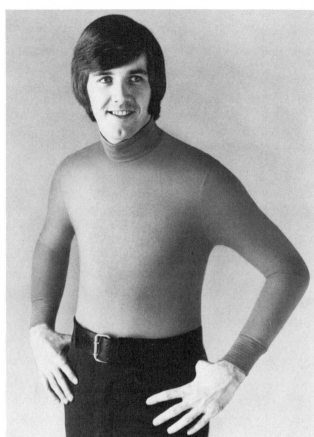

Fig.4-8

Fig.4-9

Rugged Wear makes beautiful classic 100% cotton rugby shirts with a very heavy and dense knit. Made in Narragansett, R.I., on old reconverted sweater-knitting machines, these shirts have a tight weave twill collar and super-durable rubber buttons. Seams are excellently finished. Tough and handsome, it should take you a long time to wear out one of these. This company also makes great cotton gabardine shorts and will soon be offering pants as well. Available nationally or from Rugged Wear. $36. **(Fig. 4-7)**

100% Duofold turtlenecks have spandex in collar and cuffs for shape retention and an extra long body. The special two-way stretch shoulder seam is designed to lessen stress where holes frequently occur in most other turtlenecks. Available nationally or from Norm Thompson. $15. **(Fig. 4-8)**

The Sonora Shirt is made in Mexico of 100% cotton, hand loomed for a distinctive texture. Full-cut sleeves and body allow ease of movement. Available from Early Winters. $19. **(Fig. 4-9)**

Medico 100% cotton turtlenecks, made in West Germany from top-quality long staple cotton, have a very high reputation. Elasticized collar and cuffs reportedly hold their shape through repeated washings. We haven't had a chance to try them but we've been hearing very good reports.

Medico also offers a zip-neck model that allows you to open the neck into a collar or close it up into a turtleneck. Set-in yoke at neck ensures best fit when worn in either position. Both models available from The Ski Hut. $18. Zip-neck, $23. **(Fig. 4-10)**

Fig.4-10

Fig.4-12

Fig.4-11

Soft 100% cotton pinwale corduroy shirt with rounded collar, mock tortoiseshell buttons, and tartan lining at neck, under collar and pocket flap, and at cuffs. Available from Norm Thompson. $50.   **(Fig. 4-11)**

Chamois cloth camouflage shirt for those of you who like to keep a low profile. Available from Eddie Bauer. $22.
(Fig. 4-12)

Men's and women's desert cloth shirts of polyester and long staple cotton have extra long shirt tails. Available from Eddie Bauer. Short sleeved, $20. Long sleeved, $21.
(Fig. 4-13)

Fig. 4-13

Fig.4-14

Classic shirts made of fine Battenkill flannel, woven in Switzerland of 80% cotton, 20% wool. Long tails stay tucked in. These are shirts to consider seriously for men and women. Orvis also carries some nice-looking Viyella shirts of 55% Merino wool and 45% long staple pima cotton. Available from Orvis. Battenkill, $43. Viyella, $55.

(Fig. 4-14)

Fishnet T-shirts. Worn under a close-fitting shirt, mesh construction traps warm body air yet allows moisture to evaporate. In warm weather, wear alone for full ventilation. Available from L. L. Bean. White, $6.50. Colors, $8.

(Fig. 4-15)

Hathaway is definitely one of the finest men's and women's branded shirt companies in America. Their dedication to quality craftsmanship is exemplary. They use single-needle tailoring on all their seams; full interlined plackets on shirt front and cuffs; extra long shirt tails to stay tucked in; very neatly finished buttonholes that won't unravel in the wash; three-hole buttons, a Hathaway symbol, are designed to withstand the ravages of time. Patterned fabrics are precisely matched, including the extra large pocket. Collars are handmade and the points reinforced with an extra patch of material for neatness and longer wear. Each shirt is embroidered with a red H on the bottom front of the shirt tail so even when a Hathaway shirt is sold under a private label, you can still recognize it as a Hathaway. Available nationally, or for a local source, inquire: C. F. Hathaway Co., 90 Park Ave., New York, N.Y. 10016 (212) 697-5566.

Pendleton is an old name but one that continues to live up to its deserved reputation. Among their other wool clothing, Pendleton makes a fine line of 100% virgin wool shirts. Available nationally.

One day while trudging through a trade show, we suddenly came upon some fantastic shirts. They were Dakota shirts, created by an inspired fellow named Alan Rosanes. Alan designs each shirt himself, from the yarn to the fabric. All are 100% long staple cotton, meticulously constructed and classically designed. Alan frowns upon shortcuts and flash-in-the-pan styling. He also makes a beautiful line of sweaters and pants. Definitely a name to look out for. For a local source, inquire: Dakota, 1411 Broadway, New York, N.Y. 10018.

The quality of many knit shirts has been falling off drastically. One company that was repeatedly recommended to us is Cross Creek. Indeed, upon inspection of their goods, we were duly impressed. Their knit shirts are all knit full fashion, of either 100% two-ply long staple mercerized cotton or a polyester/cotton blend. They use a patented process of shrink- and wrinkle-resistance which ensures that Cross Creek shirts will not shrink out of size. Available nationally.

Skyr and/or Scandia is another very good brand for high-quality 100% cotton turtlenecks and other knit tops. Available nationally.

Fig.4-15

TROUSERS

Here are the basic quality points to check for:

Look for a generous center back outlet seam for easy alterations. The waistband should also be seamed at the same place.

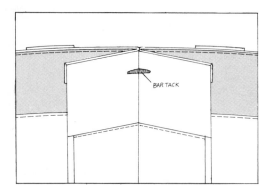

Center back outlet seam

A gently curved waistband will conform to your body and fit more comfortably; it should be securely attached and the ends neatly finished. The waistband should be reinforced with stiffeners to prevent its rolling over. A shirt-gripper liner will help shirts stay tucked in.

Belt loops which are set into the waistband seam at both top and bottom are the strongest construction. Bar tacking at both top and bottom is essential.

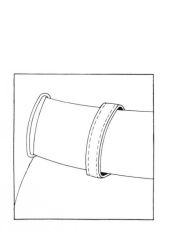
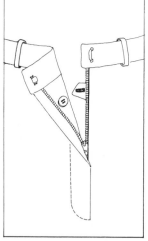

Inset belt loop   **Double closure**

This double closure is a safety feature and also makes pants "sit" better. A permanently secured metal hook and eye does not allow for minor waistband fit adjustments but, if of good quality, it has the advantage that it cannot be broken at the laundry.

The front placket in a well-designed pair of pants is curved to conform to your shape. Look for a self-locking zipper pull tab and double-stitched zipper tape. Aluminum zippers are junky in our opinion and don't belong on a quality garment. Look for brass, or nylon. The zipper should be bar tacked at top and bottom of placket across the seamline to prevent seam from ripping. A third bar tack is sometimes seen on rugged pants at the base of the zipper, which reduces the strain on the bottom stop. Check finish work around bottom of placket and crotch; because many seams join in this area, it is tricky to do neatly. All seams should be cleanly finished.

Pocket linings should be of a durable, tightly woven material, whether cotton, nylon, or a blend. Manufacturers often use cheaper fabrics in hidden areas; if pockets are stiff and boardy, quite possibly the fabric is loosely woven with a starchy filler added. After a few washings, all the filler will be gone and you'll be left with a piece of cheesecloth. Examine the material carefully.

Pocket linings should be stitched first at the bottom, turned inside out to put the raw edges inside, then sewn again so no raw edges are left exposed. An adequate alternative is a single row of stitches with the raw edges overcast. Pockets should be bar tacked at the top and bottom of the opening. Pocket facing (of the outside fabric) should be sufficiently generous that the pocket lining does not show when you sit down or once the pockets start to gap slightly with use.

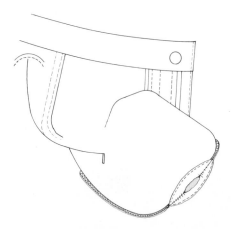

Side pocket inside

On a yoke construction, all seams should align neatly where they meet. Poor alignment is a sure sign of poor quality control and may well mean other areas of the garment are equally sloppy.

Linings reduce bagging at knees and seat, provide extra warmth, and prevent any itchiness of wool. Linings can also cover up poor workmanship in the pants; check under the lining, particularly around waistband and crotch area.

Fig.4-16

TROUSER SOURCES

Sportif is a good company that specializes exclusively in pants and shorts, although we hear they may be introducing a shirt design in the future. Sportif's workmanship and attention to detail and quality construction are excellent. Their designs are sound and well thought out.

Although Sportif works with a range of top-grade cloths, John Kirsch, the company's guiding spirit, has specially developed Espa-Plus, a stretch fabric using a blend of cotton and polyester wrapped around a central core of spandex.

The six-pocket shorts have 32 separate bar tacks. Their bike shorts are terry-cloth lined inside the seat. They use a contoured waistband on all pants and shorts for comfort and superior fit.

Great stuff, but beware of imitators. As far as we know, there's only one Sportif.

Available from Eddie Bauer, L. L. Bean, Land's End, Holubar, and The Ski Hut.

Sportif 100% cotton corduroy bib shorts. $23. **(Fig. 4-16)**

Six-pocket shorts. $29. **(Fig. 4-17)**

Fig.4-17

Six-pocket pants in stretch Espa-Plus for men and women. $48.   **(Fig. 4-18)**

Craghoppers, by H. Pickles and Sons, are imported from England. Developed specifically for mountain climbers, these pants are made of a hard-wearing Derby tweed using a tough blend of 65% wool, with nylon, rayon, and cotton. Real rugged pocket material; reinforced shirt-gripper waistband; inset belt loops for extra strength. For a local source, inquire: Climb High, 227 Main St., Burlington Vt. 05401. $59.   **(Fig. 4-19)**

These pants sure beat those hip-hugging designer monstrosities. Judging from the top-quality, industrial-weight 100% cotton fabrics, Unjeans pants and shorts will give you real value at a reasonable price. Cut roomy, with an adjustable drawcord waist. Triple-stitched along major seams; double-stitched everywhere else. Choice of 14 oz. canvas duck, double-filled, or 10 oz. high-thread count sateen. Fabric is prewashed and preshrunk. Also available in shorts. Available from Norm Thompson and Early Winters. $29.   **(Fig. 4-20)**

Fig.4-18

Fig.4-19

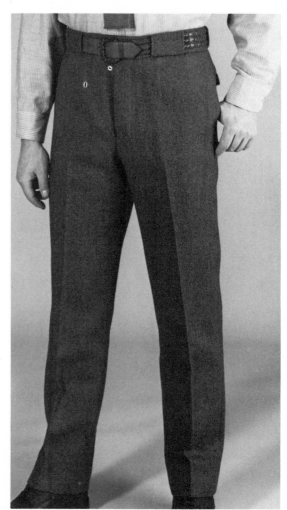

Fig.4-20

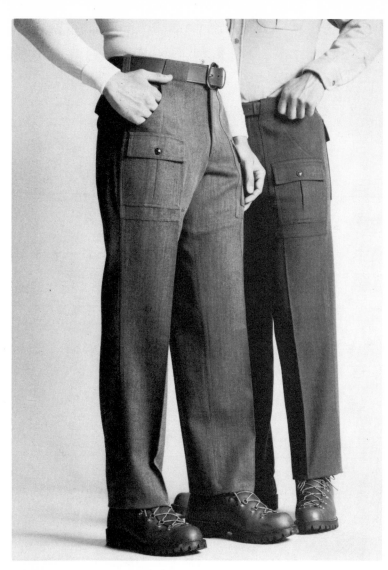

Fig.4-21

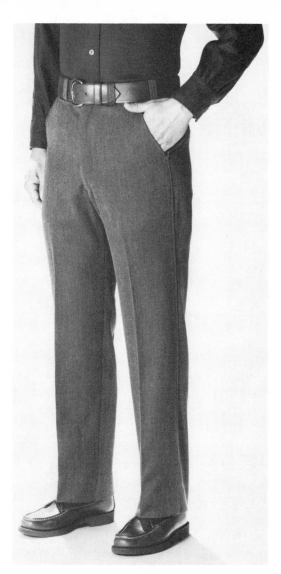

Fig.4-22

Fig.4-23

The C. C. Filson Company has been delivering top-quality clothing since 1897. Garments manufactured 30 or 40 years ago are practically identical to those being made today. Filson has had many imitators but none, as far as we know, has ever matched the quality and outstanding value that Filson steadfastly delivers.

Designed specifically for the logger and outdoorsman, Filson uses only the most durable 100% virgin wool and cotton fabrics obtainable, much of it manufactured exclusively to their own rigorous specifications. This is particularly true of their 100% virgin wool serge, known in the Northwest as the "Alaska Tuxedo" material.

Their whipcord trousers are just unbelievably rugged and handsome. We've seen them go through a rainstorm and then a grueling day at the office and come through holding their crease with nary a wrinkle. For the goods delivered, their prices are very fair. If only other companies in the country took their lead from Filson.

Available from C. C. Filson, Eddie Bauer, and Orvis.

Filson Backpacker pants for men and women. All wool worsted whipcord. Roomy cargo pockets with pleated bellows top pocket. $59. **(Fig. 4-21)**

Filson Whipcord pants of 100% worsted wool whipcord. $55. **Fig. 4-22)**

Herringbone tweed trousers are lined with 100% cotton 3/4-length lining to protect against irritation. Lining also provides extra warmth. Two deep front slash pockets. Available from Norm Thompson. $65. **(Fig. 4-23)**

Cavalry twill, with its classic diagonal weave, has a long-standing reputation for wearing like iron. Of 100% virgin wool, these slacks have cleanly finished seams, bar tacking at all stress points, and a heavy-duty locking zipper. Extra deep pocket facing for neat appearance. Available from Norm Thompson. $75. **(Fig. 4-24)**

100% worsted wool dress trousers for women. Cut straight from waist to ankle. Front watch pocket and back pocket in addition to side pockets let into seams. Available from Norm Thompson. $65. **(Fig. 4-25)**

Fig. 4-24

Fig. 4-25

Denim briar pants are faced with 400 denier nylon—no more ripped out knees. Available from Orvis. $29. **(Fig. 4-26)**

Patagonia Clothing is made by Great Pacific Ironworks, a company originally founded by Yvon Chouinard, the famous mountaineer. Although Great Pacific Ironworks specializes in supplying climbing hardware, they saw a need for tough, practical clothing and so the Patagonia line was born.

Corduroy trousers made from very rugged 100% cotton corduroy woven in England. Two large front pockets, two tab closure back pockets. Available from Great Pacific. $42. **(Fig. 4-27)**

Twill trousers developed with hot weather in mind. The 100% cotton twill fabric is very lightweight but strong. Pants are cut wide for freedom of movement and comfort on sultry days. Two rear flap pockets; two on-seam side pockets. Available from Great Pacific. $29. **(Fig. 4-28)**

Canvas trousers of 11 oz. 100% cotton duck. Two tab closure rear pockets; two deep front pockets. Available from Great Pacific. $24. **(Fig. 4-29)**

Duck shorts of 100% cotton canvas are cut short and wide for easy movement and good ventilation on hot days. Four deep pockets. Available from Great Pacific or The Ski Hut. $20. **(Fig. 4-30)**

In our estimation, Arthur Winer is definitely one of the best pants makers you'll ever find. The company makes pants and only pants so they get plenty of practice. Arthur Winer, however, rarely sells under its own name; instead, Winer sells to the better stores across the country who sew in their own private labels. If the salesperson can assure you it's Arthur Winer, then you know you've got a good garment. You just have to ask around.

Fig.4-26

Fig.4-27

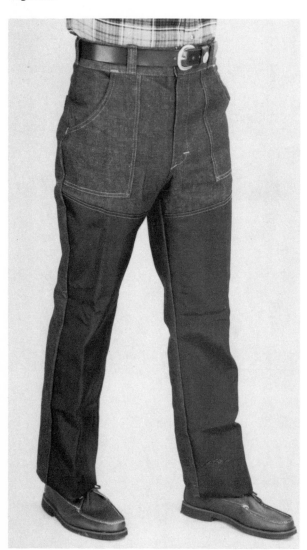

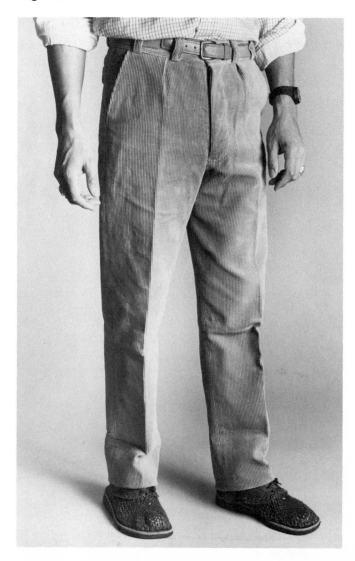

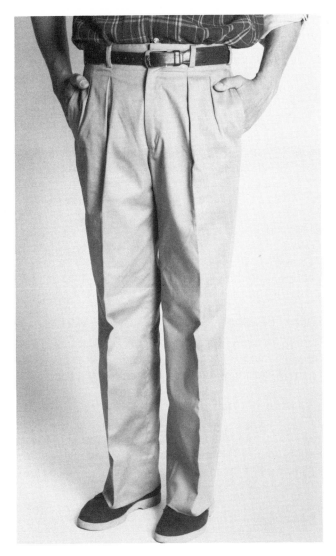

Fig. 4-28

Fig. 4-29

Fig. 4-30

SWEATERS

Here are the basic quality points to check for:

"Full fashion" in knit garments is an indication of good quality. The various sections, such as body, sleeves, and collar, are knitted to shape by increasing or decreasing the number of stitches, rather than being cut to shape. As a result, all garment parts have finished edges and all seams are then preferably knitted, instead of sewed, together. Full fashion is a better quality construction because the shaping of the garment is permanent and will not distort during washing. Also, if side seams were to come unstitched, there are no cut edges to run or unravel.

The small alterations in the knit caused by the change in the position of the yarn as stitches are added or decreased are called "fashion marks." Mock fashion marks, usually produced by embroidery, are sometimes employed to give the appearance of a better garment. Do not be fooled.

Very inexpensive and poor-quality sweaters are not only cut and sewn, but the knit fabric has also often been stretched out before cutting to achieve maximum yardage. When washed, the material "relaxes" again, in other

 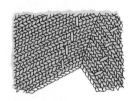

Fashion marks   **Mock fashion marks**

words, shrinks substantially, and you end up with a sweater just about large enough to fit a newborn hamster.

Incidentally, when sweaters pill, do not cut off the pills. Pull them off gently or stroke lengthwise with a sweater comb or a clean, dry sponge.

OILED WOOL SWEATERS

Oiled wool is more water-repellent than regular wool which has had most of its natural lanolin removed. Oiled wool garments should never be dry cleaned because this will remove all the oil. Gently hand wash as you would any fine wool sweater.

As with most things, there are *oiled* wool sweaters and then there are *oiled* wool sweaters. The genuine article has never had its natural oils removed; it is knitted in this greasy state. With facsimile oiled wool sweaters, the wool has been scoured clean, removing all the oil; it is knitted in this clean state; and the finished sweater is then *sprayed* with

oil. These sweaters lose their oil fairly rapidly. The genuine articles will never completely lose their oil if you treat them carefully.

Wash an oiled wool sweater as seldom as possible. Hand wash gently, using a minimum amount of soap, not detergent. Each time you wash the sweater, it will probably get a little softer and fluffier, and each time some of the oil will have been removed. In New Zealand, the sweater would be rubbed over the back of a sheep to replenish the oils. A more convenient alternative is to add a little vegetable oil to the final rinse water.

Some diehards would never dream of washing their oiled wools at all, preferring to revel in the friendly, familiar scent of a trusty old sweater.

SWEATER SOURCES

So many of the mountaineers we interviewed mentioned Dachstein that we bought ourselves a couple. They're not cheap but what a sweater! You're not buying just a sweater—it's a family heirloom.

Produced in Austria by Herr Derkogner who got his start making mittens to sell locally back in 1913, all Dachstein products are knitted from 100% oiled gray virgin wool which is specially shrunk to produce a very dense and extremely durable garment while retaining its soft texture. Highly water-repellent and windproof, it's like wearing a cozy jacket. Available from International Mountain Equipment and Harborside. $170.   **(Fig. 4-31)**

The French Creek Sheep and Wool Company, famous for its first-rate shearling coats, also offers a superb line of greasewool sweaters. They shear and spin much of their wool from their own sheep and their policy is always to make the finest they know how. The wool is top-grade long staple Corriedale with the natural lanolin left in to give better protection against wind and rain. Fully fashioned in an unusual heavy rib, the seams are hand crocheted; buttonholes are machine stitched for strength, then hand finished. The more these sweaters are washed, the softer they feel and the purer the color. Available in 1-ply to 4-ply weights for all weather conditions, and in a wide selection of original designs. By all odds, these are some of the finest sweaters made in the United States.

French Creek Lady's raglan sweater coat: 4-ply greasewool with capacious collar which can be worn open or buttoned up. Patch pockets, epaulets, buckled sash belt, and suede elbow patches. Also shown is 80″ long fringed muffler and knit cap. $265.   **(Fig. 4-32)**

Fig.4-31

Fig.4-32

Fig.4-33

French Creek short sweater coat: 4-ply greasewool, double-thick shawl collar. Hand-sewn suede elbow patches, leather buttons. $170.   **(Fig. 4-33)**

Another unique French Creek offering. Sweaters of 100% natural unscoured cotton, mercerized for strength and texture. As with all French Creek garments, expertly crafted. Also available is a ladies' and men's cotton polo pullover and ladies' short sleeve scoop neck model. Vest, $42. Turtleneck, $50. Crew, $50.   **(Fig. 4-34)**

Sweaters by Bergman use 100% virgin wool, are machine washable and dryable, water- and stain-repellent, and moth proofed. Cuffs and ribbing are doubled for extra wear. Generously sized for roomy fit. Hand-crafted in southern New Hampshire from original designs. Available from Bergman and L. L. Bean. $60.   **(Fig. 4-35)**

Fig.4-34

Fig.4-35

Fig.4-36

Fig.4-37

Fig.4-38

Fig.4-39

100% cotton natural-color sweaters. Available from David Morgan. Crew, $28. Turtleneck, $23.   **(Fig. 4-36)**

Traditional Guernsey sweater is very tightly knit of a tough worsted yarn. Hand-framed and full-fashioned, the bottom has a sturdy double hem and side vents to ensure the bottom won't roll up. Special gussets at neck and under the arm ensure comfortable fit and add years to the life of the garment. Available from David Morgan. $83.   **(Fig. 4-37)**

This Australian Jumbuk sweater is made from Corriedale oiled wool for long wear and good water resistance. The sweater is knit with a thick stitch and the boatneck design provides a 5″ wide double layer across the shoulders and around the neck, a great asset because this area tends to be compressed or stretched in use. Generously sized. Available from David Morgan. $66.   **(Fig. 4-38)**

Knit in Ireland from the natural brown fleece of Icelandic sheep, the wool for this cardigan has not been bleached or dyed. It retains its natural lanolin, giving it additional water repellency. Leather buttons and two pockets. Available from Orvis. $90.   **(Fig. 4-39)**

Fig.4-40

Fig.4-41

Fig.4-42

Fig. 4-43

Fig. 4-44

All-cotton cardigan sweater. Something a little different but still most practical. A classic V-neck with two front pockets. Sweater has spandex knitted into collar, cuff, and waistband ribbing for shape retention. Very nice indeed. Available from Orvis. $37. **(Fig. 4-40)**

Black sheep sweater for men and women. Knitted in Ireland from the gray-black wool of Icelandic sheep. Available from Orvis. $88. **(Fig. 4-41)**

100% Sea Island cotton sweater, made in England. Cotton this quality is a rare bird these days. Available from Norm Thompson. $50. **(Fig. 4-42)**

Hand knit Aran Islands sweater made from undyed black sheep wool, actually an ash-gray color. Large collar turns up for extra protection against the chill. An unusual and extremely handsome sweater. Available from Norm Thompson. $95. **(Fig. 4-43)**

Harris Tweed sweater. Knit of pure wool on the Island of Jersey, this sweater combines front panels of Harris tweed with an all-knit back for ease of movement. An attractive and unusual marriage. Bellows pockets provide plenty of carrying space. Warm enough to wear as a jacket as well as a sweater. Available from Norm Thompson. $120.

(Fig. 4-44)

Fig.4-45

Fig.4-46

Fig.4-47

Fig.4-48

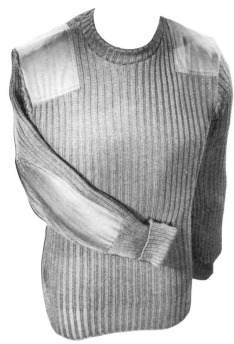

Fig.4-51

Fig.4-49

Royal Robbins is another highly respected mountaineer outfitter. Mr. Robbins himself is a famous figure in climbing. He has a collection of mountain wear which is composed principally of beautiful, beefy 100% virgin wool sweaters, many imported from Great Britain and Uruguay. We haven't had the pleasure of trying any of his sweaters but Robbins comes with first-class credentials. Available from Royal Robbins. $26–$90. **(Figs. 4-45, 46, 47, 48)**

Kalpakian Knitting Mills are well spoken of. They manufacture a wide variety of functionally attractive 100% virgin wool sweaters. Also socks and knit caps. Available from Kalpakian. Sweaters, $70–$150. Socks $15–$20.
(Fig. 4-49)

Norsewear makes some excellent pure virgin wool sweaters imported from New Zealand. Available from Land's End, Marmot, Holubar, and Sierra Designs. For more information, contact: Norsewear, P.O. Box 1263/249 Little Falls Road, Fairfield, N.J. 07006 (201) 785-2355. $50–$100. **(Fig. 4-50)**

Wooly Pully, the original British Commando sweater of 100% virgin wool. Manufactured exactly to British Ministry of Defense specifications. There are many knockoffs of this classic sweater floating around but this is the genuine article. Tightly woven polyester/cotton twill reinforcing patches over shoulders and forearm. Also available in V-neck and mock turtleneck. Available from Brigade Quartermaster. $50. **(Fig. 4-51)**

Fig.4-50

SPORTS JACKETS, SUITS, AND VESTS

Here are the basic quality points to check for in jackets:

A well-made, properly fitting jacket requires a great deal of skill and labor to make. Much of the workmanship you never see—you just feel it in the comfort and ease of the jacket. Pressing as each individual step is completed is an essential component in the final quality of the jacket.

You can *feel* a good fit but here are some points to look for. Lapels and collars should fold over with a gentle roll, rather than a sharp crease. The front neckline should fit snugly and the lapels should lie smoothly over the chest with no gapping. The back of the neck should rest smoothly on your collar and not gap away from your neck.

The shoulder line from neck to shoulder point should lie smoothly without bunching and there should be no pull or strain across the shoulders in the back. The soft or natural shoulder, as opposed to padded shoulder, is the most versatile and enduring style. Look also for moderate lapel shapes.

Armholes that are cut too deeply will restrict arm movement; they should be cut only deep enough so as not to bind. Regardless of the cut, when you raise your arms, the coat will lift up slightly.

There are certain other quality points to look for. Seam edges should be bound or carefully overcast. Check under the lining to make sure its seams, too, are also cleanly finished. If the jacket is fully lined, feel through the lining with your hands to judge how the seam edges have been finished.

Oxford suits, considered by many the finest suits to be had, are only half-lined. Mr. Jack McDonald, the president, believes full linings are used to cover up sloppy workmanship. In jackets that are not fully lined, there should be a lining over the pockets and vents.

If the jacket is fully lined, as is common on most women's jackets, the lining should be secured at sleeve and shoulder area, at armholes and sideseams, and also at the sleeve bottom to prevent the lining from peeking past the cuff. It should fit without wrinkling or bagging at the armholes and cuff, and should hang freely at the hem without pulling at the outer fabric. A small horizontal pleat at the jacket hem will allow greater freedom of movement and, for the same reason, there should also be a vertical center pleat in the back. Hand-stitching the lining at this back pleat and around the armholes provides more "give" than would machine-stitching.

The felt undercollar lining should be color-matched or color-coordinated and stitched by hand along its bottom edge.

Pocket flaps, except perhaps on very heavy fabrics, should be self-lined for neatness. Pocket linings should be of durable, tightly woven material. Make sure, especially on women's jackets, that the manufacturer has not skimped by omitting inside pockets—these are invaluable. Generous bellows pockets, when you can find them, are always a plus.

Buttons should be sewn on firmly and mounted on a stem or a thread shank. Buttonholes should be keyhole shape and closely whipstitched to stand up to wear. Look at the backside of the buttonhole to make sure both sides have been cleanly finished. Buttonholes are sometimes stitched by hand for more flexibility than a machine can provide.

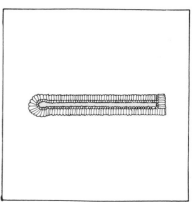

Keyhole buttonhole

SPORTS JACKET AND SUIT SOURCES

Philip Van Erin is a recent name specializing in women's classic clothing, although they have recently added a men's line as well. A small company, run by Philip Vallieres and his wife Linda, it is dedicated to setting a standard of excellence and, from everything we've seen, it is right on target. Here is something for the mass-produced schlock masters to reckon with.

Soft shoulder classic styling, well-fitted across the back and neck, featuring Harris tweed and other fine cloths, with a great deal of hand-sewn work, Van Erin jackets, pants, and skirts are a wise investment.

Van Erin women's clothes are not just rehashed versions of men's wear. For example, on the jacket, the inside pocket is neatly placed to fit into the hollow between a woman's hip bone and her stomach.

Van Erin clothing is sometimes sold under a store's own private label. For a local source, inquire: Philip Van Erin Inc., 8 West 40 Street, New York, N.Y. 10018 (212) 354-1114.

One of Van Erin's fine women's jackets. $200. Men's jackets, $175. **(Fig. 4-52)**

Women's suit made of tough, traditional Nailshead tweed of 100% worsted wool and fully lined with acetate. Skirt has back zipper and two pockets set into side seams. Jacket has slightly padded shoulders and inside pocket. Available from Norm Thompson. $235. **(Fig. 4-53)**

Ladies' hacking suit and men's hacking jacket of Harris Tweed. Both fully lined, with suede elbow patches and leather buttons. Available from French Creek. Ladies' jacket, $230. Skirt, $155. Men's jacket, $195. **(Fig. 4-54)**

Fig.4-52

Fig.4-53

Fig.4-54

Fig.4-55

Fig.4-56

Jacket of 100% finest quality camel hair for lightweight warmth. Classic styling; three inside pockets. Uncommon by today's standards. Available from Norm Thompson. $250. **(Fig. 4-55)**

Classically styled sports jacket of Connemara tweed, hand woven in Ireland. Available from Norm Thompson. $160. **(Fig. 4-56)**

Bladen Brothers of England is tough to find over here but well worth looking for. They make very fine quality clothing. This is the Essex style jacket with bellows pockets and bi-swing back. Some Bladen hacking jackets are carried by Mayfield Saddlery, The Cambridge Bldg., Suite 5B, 208 South Pulaski St., Baltimore, Md. 21223 (301) 233-2420. **(Fig. 4-57)**

Filson's Forestry Cloth Cruiser and Pants. Made from a beautiful textured 100% wool worsted serge. Lightweight and rugged. Jacket has button front, four generous snap-closure front pockets, and large utility pocket tactfully designed into the back. Pants are full cut and nicely tailored, with four deep, roomy pockets plus watch pocket. Available from C. C. Filson. Cruiser, $105. Pants, $64. **(Fig. 4-58)**

Vest tailored in England of brown and gray check Harris Tweed. Lined with 100% viscose rayon. Leather bound pockets, genuine horn buttons. Orvis also has a very nice line of Harris Tweed jackets and pants, with swatches available on request. Available from Orvis. $49. **(Fig.4-59)**

Sueded pigskin vest, fully rayon lined, with genuine bone buttons. Available from L. L. Bean. $52. **(Fig. 4-60)**

Southwick and Arthur Freedberg are fine names in men's and women's jackets and suits. Well-tailored, carefully constructed, and free from trendy styling. With these names, you pay for the quality, not for a fancy label. Available nationally.

Fig.4-57

Fig.4-58

Fig.4-60

Fig.4-59

CAMBRIAN FLY FISHERS AND RATCATCHER CLOTHING

Cambrian Fly Fishers and Ratcatcher clothing is unparalleled in our experience. Thank heaven they found their way over here from England. This country has nothing quite like them.

Mr. S. J. Diggory, the company's founder and guiding spirit, settles for nothing but the best and insists not only on quality but superb value in exchange for dollars received. And does he deliver! We just can't say enough good things about this company. You really have to see their clothing to fully appreciate it.

Mr. Diggory, who is an inveterate outdoorsman and sporting enthusiast, was, in his earlier days, a racing car driver but elected to get out of it while, as he puts it, "his skin was still whole." He decided to apply his acute talents for engineering and precision planning to clothing, with exemplary success.

Cambrian, among other things, specializes in Grade A primo moleskin clothing. Rugged, soft, completely washable, requiring little or no ironing, 100 percent cotton, and probably the finest in the world.

According to Mr. Diggory, moleskin pants that are worn every day under punishing conditions by English gamekeepers and washed once a week, last five years. The rugged moleskin sports jacket and pants are so handsome together that they are as at home in an office overlooking Park Avenue as in the bush country for which they were originally designed.

Pockets and waistband are of strong synthetic fabric. Mr. Diggory feels that bar tacks are "a sign of defeat," saying that a properly constructed garment has no need of extra reinforcement at stress points.

Cambrian makes excellent corduroy garments, cut with the nap facing down to shed the rain, as well as cavalry twills.

In the Fall of 1980, Mr. Diggory expects to present his Alaskan Ratcatcher pants. Extremely warm, they will be one-third the weight of moleskin and also machine-washable, made of cotton with a silk lining and an interlining. He is working on clothing for tropical conditions as well.

Mr. Diggory has a very simple return policy: He will always replace a garment without question.

Available from Cambrian Fly Fishers.

Fig.4-61

 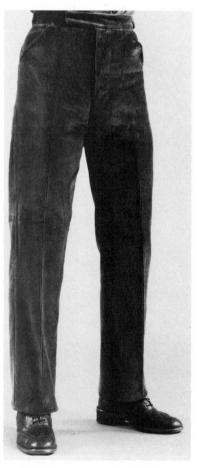

Fig.4-62

Fig.4-63

Ratcatcher moleskin vest with leather bound pockets and rayon lining. Available from Orvis. $65.   **(Fig. 4-61)**

Men's heavyweight corduroy trousers made of exceptionally fine and gutsy corduroy of 100% cotton. Self-supporting waist. Women's version available in slightly lighter-weight corduroy. Men's, $82. Women's $83.   **(Fig. 4-62)**

Men's and women's moleskin shirts made of a lighter-weight moleskin. Soft and comfortable to wear. We'd opt for these over a flannel or chamois cloth shirt. $45. **(Fig.4-63)**

Rain choker. Looking for a functional ascot? You've got it. Made from especially fine and highly absorbent face-cloth-weight terry cloth. No more rain down your neck, good for wiping your face, and warm too. $8.   **(Fig. 4-64)**

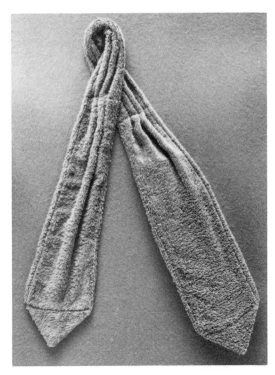

Fig.4-64

Fig.4-65

Fig.4-66

Fowler jackets, available in lightweight and heavyweight versions. Made of rugged cotton wax-impregnated for waterproofness. Both have corduroy collar with foldaway lined hood; two-way zipper; two large bellows pockets and two side slash pockets. Lightweight, $165. Heavyweight, $182.   **(Fig. 4-65)**

Men's and women's ribbed matchlock sweater of 100% wool. Suede leather patches. Shown with women's moleskin trousers. $80.   **(Fig. 4-66)**

British Khaki is a very unusual company. Mr. Robert Lighton traveled to India and found the original mill and factory that produced much of the field wear for the British Army. It's no secret that the British Army dressed in the best.

Mr. Lighton is now reviving a tradition that we had feared was gone forever. At the heart of his success is the excellent all-cotton fabrics he uses; drill cloth, poplin, and heavy duck. We have a few pairs of the original military British Gurkha pants; a comparison of this Gurkha cloth with his cloth indicates that Mr. Lighton's is actually superior.

All of the British Khaki garments are derived from classic designs: functional and to the point. He makes excellent safari jackets, fine poplin shirts, a variety of pants, and some very well-done field jackets and coats. For men and women. To the best of our knowledge no one else has access to these quality fabrics, so don't be misled by possible imitations. British Khaki is in a class by itself. It's definitely a label to keep your eyes peeled for.

Available nationally, or for a local source, inquire: British Khaki, 730 Fifth Avenue, New York, N.Y. 10019.

FLIGHT SUITS

Flight Suits Ltd. is definitely a unique company. We know of no one else like them anywhere. There are a few other flight-suit makers around the country but none that deliver anywhere near such high quality and custom design capabilities.

Jim Wegge, President and guiding spirit, makes men's and women's flight suits, jackets, shirts, and pants, *custom-tailored* only. He also makes 100 percent Nomex flight suits and auto racing suits. Although Mr. Wegge works from several basic designs, he's always happy to accommodate a customer's design modifications. Don't worry about becoming exotic—he'll deliver just about anything you want, within reason.

Flight Suits is pleased to take orders by mail and their catalog contains detailed instructions on how to take your measurements. They offer a wide range of color choices but if you have a special fabric you want used, just mail it along with your order. They offer a "satisfaction unconditionally guaranteed" fit. Prices are very reasonable.

Fig. 4-68

Fig. 4-67

The standard men's flight suit, available in long or short sleeved versions, has two large zippered chest pockets and two zippered chart pockets on the legs. An expansion back pleat allows freedom of movement; an elastic back waistband and adjustable Velcro-fastened front belt ensures a comfortable fit. All flight suits have sewn-through trouser creases and all seams are double top-stitched. Long sleeved flight suit has a zippered bellows pocket on the upper arm with attached pen and pencil pocket, whereas short sleeved suits have pen and pencil pocket only. $84. **(Fig. 4-67)**

Women's standard flight suit has all the same construction features as the men's suit. The standard suit has either a belt fastened in the center with Velcro or a tie belt. $94. **(Fig. 4-68)**

Fig.4-69

Fig.4-70

Here's an example of some of the customizing that's possible. Custom work usually runs $20–$30 extra.
(Fig. 4-69)

Flight jacket has either knitted or self-fabric collar, cuffs, and waistband. It comes lined or unlined. Front expansion pockets are available either single or double on each side. Optional zippered bellows pocket on sleeve. $49. **(Fig.4-70)**

UNDERWEAR

The consultants we talked with have consistently recommended Duofold as a high caliber source. Our phone conversations with this company have reflected their definite strong concern with integrity and quality.

We were both impressed by their men's 100 percent cotton underwear. A lot of cotton briefs are pretty badly designed and don't hold up well under long-term use. But Duofold seems to be a cut above and then some.

Duofold is probably most famous for their insulated underwear. They use a dual layer of cotton and wool; cotton on the inside for tactile comfort and virgin wool blended with cotton and nylon on the outside. They are well-shaped and designed so as to fit most comfortably under your clothing, with a variety of styles and weights to meet your specific needs. Machine washable. You may have to pay a bit more but in our opinion, you get a whole lot more. Available nationally.

Knitted boxer shorts of 100% combed and mercerized cotton by Duofold. Available from Norm Thompson. $6.50
(Fig. 4-71)

Norse-Net shirt of 50% cotton, 50% polyester. $9.
(Fig. 4-72)

Classic Duofold two-piece long underwear. We feel that two-piece long johns are more versatile. Top, $12. Bottom $12.
(Fig. 4-73)

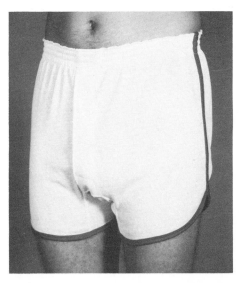

Fig.4-71

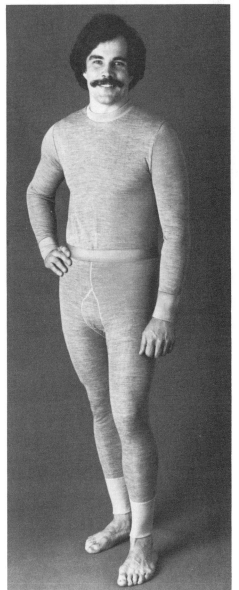

Fig.4-73

Fig.4-72

Fig.4-74

"Wallace Beery" undershirt with button placket front. Inner fabric is 100% cotton, outer fabric is a blend of 40% wool, 50% cotton, and 10% nylon. Available from The Ski Hut. $14.   **(Fig. 4-74)**

Silk underwear for the practical-minded hedonist. Top also available long sleeved. Available from Orvis. Short-sleeved, $41. Long sleeved, $45. Bottoms, $64.   **(Fig. 4-75)**

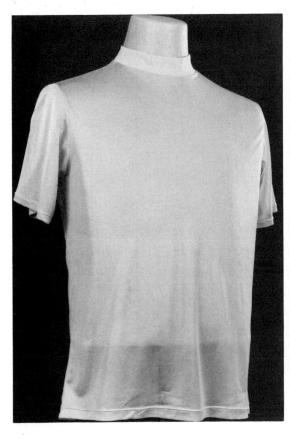
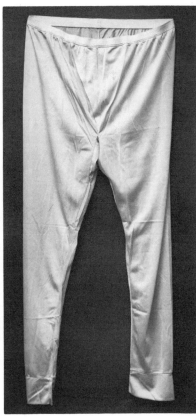

Fig.4·75

SOCKS

For outdoor enthusiasts, especially mountain climbers, sock selection can become a rather complicated business. Fortunately, for daily street-wear conditions, considerations regarding socks are more straightforward.

Wear and comfort are the two major factors. Pure natural fiber socks, be they wool, cotton, or silk, do not wear as well as man-mades or blends. We've found, contrary to popular folk wisdom and advertising propaganda, that certain 100 percent man-made socks can be exceptionally comfortable, even on torrid summer days.

One word of caution—in cold weather, don't wear socks so thick that they make your shoes fit tightly. Tight shoes make for cold feet because they reduce circulation. Remember, as we explained earlier, slightly cool feet have been scientifically shown to encourage and promote overall body warmth.

Changing your socks on a frequent, preferably daily, basis is most desirable, mainly because accumulation of perspiration, dirt, and microscopic organisms in your shoes rots the leather and promotes the generation of noxious odors.

One of the most highly respected sock brands is Gold Toe, which also goes by the name Arrow. We stumbled onto them a number of years ago and have been consistently impressed with their quality. Gold Toe and Arrow make a lightweight cotton/polyester sock that wears exceptionally well. Regrettably, they only make socks for men, although this hasn't stopped a lot of women from wearing them.

Wigwam is another brand with which we have had very good experience. Among the many different and high-quality socks they manufacture, we've found one in particular very unusual. This is their 100 percent Qiana nylon liner sock. Qiana has many of the tactile properties of silk. Silk socks are extremely comfortable but are also terribly expensive and not very durable. Wigwam's Qiana sock feels luscious even in hot weather. So although your feet may be hot, which they would be in any sock, the sensual pleasure of Qiana somehow very definitely ameliorates the situation. In the winter, Wigwam Qianas can be worn under heavier wool socks to offer extra warmth and itch-free, soothing comfort. As far as we know, Wigwam is the only company presently making Qiana socks. Unfortunately, Wigwam makes them only in white. Both Gold Toe and Wigwam socks are available nationally.

5

Outerwear

OVERCOATS AND JACKETS

Overcoats and jackets conform to many of the same quality points and signs of proper fit found in sports jackets. Because outer garments are supposed to keep you warm under more rigorous conditions, there are some additional design points to look for.

A large collar (and lapels) can be turned up to protect your neck and the back of your head. A throat latch will keep it closed, leaving your hands free to clutch something other than your throat. The back vent should also be tabbed to keep it closed and it should have a good deep overlap.

A full center pleat in the lining down the back takes up the strain of wear and sateen-lined sleeves allow easy on and off. Be sure the lining is warm; an additional interlining, especially across the shoulders and back, can make all the difference. It has been our experience that man-made fleece and pile linings begin looking tacky after a relatively short time. On the other hand, good quality wool pile or alpaca pile linings wear well and maintain their good appearance.

If you are considering an all-season raincoat with a zip-in lining, try on the coat both with and without the lining—it should fit well both ways.

Knitted wristlets and a storm flap behind the front closure will keep out the elements.

Warmly lined hand-warmer pockets are a real asset when you forget your gloves. Pockets should be bar tacked at the corners. Midriff-height slash pockets (as on a peacoat) are good for walking in the rain—the angle is such that rain does not run down your sleeve and straight into the pocket.

Raglan sleeve

The armhole of a raglan sleeve must be cut carefully so as not to constrict arm movement; if cut too deep, it can keep your arms pinned by your sides. Also, if a raglan sleeve has been constructed with a center seam running across the top of the shoulder and down the sleeve, this is a potential place for rain and snow to seep in. All flat-felled shoulder seams should face *down* to prevent rain from entering.

Fig.5-1

Fig.5-2

OVERCOAT AND JACKET SOURCES:

Women's camel loden coat, imported from Austria, is made of long staple wool. It has a removable hood and a deep center pleat in the back. The lining is woven directly to the inside of the loden cloth. The men's loden coat has a raglan sleeve design and zip-close inside pocket. Available from Orvis. $430.*   **(Figs. 5-1, 2)**

*Prices listed are approximate and as of September 1980.

Gloverall of England deservedly holds a very high reputation as "coatwrights." Timeless pea coat for men and women is fully lined. Available from Norm Thompson. $135.   **(Fig. 5-3)**

Gloverall's hooded duffle coat lined with Bannockbane tartan plaid. Front and back yoke provide double thickness of fabric for extra warmth. Available from Eddie Bauer. $179.   **(Fig. 5-4)**

Fig.5-3   **Fig.5-4**

Fig.5-5

Men's llama hair stadium coat in natural camel color combines great lightweight warmth with incredible softness. Leather buttons; wool plaid lining and inside buttoned pocket. Available from French Creek. $350.   **(Fig.5-5)**

Invertere of Britain has been constantly recommended to us as we sought the names of fine clothiers. These classic, beautifully made trench coats fully live up to Invertere's reputation. The outer shell is 100% water-repellent yarn-dyed cotton; the lining is 67% polyester, 33% cotton. Full double-faced back yoke; back pleat. Deep handwarmer pockets; storm flap at neck; belted wrist adjustments and leather buckles. Available from Norm Thompson. $335.   **(Figs. 5-6, 7)**

Fig.5-6

Fig.5-7

Fig.5-8

Fig.5-9

Fig.5-10

Fig.5-11

Fig.5-13

Fig.5-12

The three Duxbak coats shown use 100% cotton, high count 2-ply, 10 oz. per square yard Army duck. Available nationally, or for local source, inquire: Utica Duxbak, 815 Noyes St., Utica, N.Y. 13502 (315) 797-0050.

Utica Duxbak style 010 and 017 double hunting coats 31″ long with self-lined body and upper sleeve. Bi-swing back and expansion game pocket in back. Corduroy-faced collar and corduroy-lined cuffs. Gusseted underarm for freer action. 010, $70. 017, $65. **(Fig. 5-8)**

Utica Duxbak style 010 has drop seat and hand-warmer pockets. **(Fig. 5-9)**

Utica Duxbak style 021 hunting coat is shorter and unlined. Drop seat game pocket in back. Corduroy collar and cuffs. Rear shoulder pleats instead of bi-swing back. $40. **(Fig. 5-10)**

Bush jacket of brushed poplin, 65% polyester/35% cotton. Available from Gokeys. $85. **(Fig. 5-11)**

Men's and women's Kingswood Sportswear golf jacket is 65% polyester/35% cotton, Zepel-treated against soil and rain. Available from Gokeys. $70. **(Fig. 5-12)**

100% cotton poplin golf jacket with tartan rayon lining; ventilated yoke back. Imported from England. Available from Gokeys. $85. **(Fig. 5-13)**

Fig.5-14

Fig.5-15

Fig.5-16

Fig. 5-17

Fig. 5-18

Berghaus 100% long staple cotton jacket is made of lightweight but high thread count canvas. Specially treated for water repellency. Nylon hood folds into zippered collar pouch. Sleeves reinforced with double fabric; knitted wristlets. Five zippered pockets and zippered front with snapclose storm flap. The only criticism we have is that the pocket zipper pulls seem a bit flimsy and too small to get a grip on, especially when wearing gloves. Available from Norm Thompson and Dennis Connor. $90.   **(Fig. 5-14)**

Norm Thompson has taken the safari jacket and transformed it into their own Shikari jacket. Made from a substantial 100% cotton twill, all inside seam edges are taped or stitched down. Sleeves and shoulders are lined for easy on and off. Double topstitching around outside seams.

Four generous bellows pockets and center back vent. Available from Norm Thompson. $115.   **(Fig. 5-15)**

Fishing shirt of 100% cotton. Four roomy front flap pockets; 12 X 11″ cargo pocket on the back and an extra pocket on the sleeve. Fleece breast patch is removable for those of you who won't be dipping your lure. Available from Orvis. $28.   **(Fig. 5-16)**

Men's and women's bush jackets are available in either 100% cotton or a 65% polyester/35% cotton blend. All have center pleat in back for ease of movement. Bellows pockets at waist and pleated expansion chest pockets. Matching bush pants. Available from Eddie Bauer. Men's, $60. Women's, $55. Bush pants, $30.   **(Figs. 5-17, 18)**

Fig.5-19

Fig.5-20

Fig.5-21

Fig.5-22

Fig.5-23

The Putney reversible jacket is 100% wool muted herringbone on one side and tan poplin of 65% polyester/35% cotton on the other side; Zepel treated for water repellency. Button cuffs, nylon drawstring in hood for snug fit. Two chest pockets and two slash pockets on wool side; chest pockets only on poplin side. Available from Norm Thompson, Orvis, and Gokeys. $70. **(Fig. 5-19)**

Lightweight, reversible Apollo jacket is made of aluminum film bonded to nylon. Silver side offers heat-reflecting capabilities. Tuck-away hood in collar pouch; drawstring waist; nylon mesh inserts under arms for ventilation. Four pockets both inside and out; pockets on silver side are zippered. Available from Norm Thompson. $49. **(Figs. 5-20, 21)**

Jacket by Swanndri of New Zealand of tightly woven 100% wool, specially treated for water repellency. Medium weight, with double yoke over shoulders and chest. Two button-down breast pockets and two slanted side pockets. Available from David Morgan. $55. **(Fig. 5-22)**

Women's llama hair reversible Windbreaker is cotton poplin on one side, soft llama hair on the other. Drawstring cuffs and hem. Available from French Creek. $264.

(Fig. 5-23)

Fig.5-24

Fig.5-26

Genuine U.S. Army M65 field coat. For the money, this is one of the best values you'll ever find. Outer shell of 50% cotton, 50% nylon. Attached hood tucks neatly into zippered collar pocket. Button-in cold weather liner optional. Available from Brigade Quartermaster. $45.   **(Fig. 5-24)**

Fig.5-25

Grenfell is one of the world's most distinguished names in raincoats, field jackets, and Windbreakers. All Grenfell garments are made of Grenfell cloth. This cloth is 100% finest long staple cotton, with an extremely tight weave of 600 threads to the square inch. The exceptionally compact weave gives Grenfell its inherent windproof, water-resistant, and long wearing qualities. The Grenfell trench coat is, in our opinion and in the opinion of some of our most demanding consultants, the finest trench coat available. This is a name to look for and invest in. For a local source, inquire of Grenfell's American importer: John M. Mendez, Inc., Suite 500, 545 Madison Ave., New York, N.Y. 10022, (212) 688-6338. Trench coat available from Dennis Connor. $400.   **(Fig. 5-25)**

Back in the early 1900s, Clinton C. Filson designed and named the famous Cruiser jacket style. The Cruiser jackets and vest, in addition to the generous front pockets, all have a large snap closing utility pocket tactfully designed into the back and an inside pocket. As Mr. Filson liked to say, "They've got more pockets than a pool table—count 'em!"

Filson is unquestionably one of the most outstanding clothing investments we've ever encountered. Filson clothes are available directly from C. C. Filson or from Eddie Bauer and Orvis.

Cruiser vest. Originally designed for loggers, this vest has a large carry pocket across the back, four front utility pockets, and two large inside pockets. Made of 10.38 oz. 100% cotton 2-ply duck or wool. Duck, $27. Wool, $30.   **(Fig. 5-26)**

Fig.5-28

Fig.5-27

Fig.5-29

Poplin Cruiser made of sturdy, lightweight 50% cotton, 50% polyester with water-repellent and stain-resistant finish. $57. **(Fig. 5-27)**

Mackinaw Cruiser of 26 oz. tightly woven 100% long staple virgin wool. A truly superb jacket. Also available for women. $93. **(Fig. 5-28)**

Double Mackinaw Cruiser: Same design as regular cruiser except that sleeves and shoulder cape are formed out of two separate layers of wool for twice the protection. 100% tightly woven long staple virgin wool. $105. **(Fig.5-29)**

Fig.5-31

Fig.5-32

Fig.5-30

Loden coat made from a superb 100% virgin wool Tyrolean loden cloth imported from Austria. Two bellows pockets, two breast slash pockets, and two inside pockets. Specially designed pivot sleeve with deep back shoulder pleats for ease of movement. Available from Cambrian Fly Fishers. $275.   **(Fig. 5-30)**

Patagonia's Range Coat. 10 oz. 100% cotton canvas with 100% wool "blanket" lining. Corduroy collar; brass buttons; triple-stitched seams. Men's has hidden side-entry hand-warmer pockets in addition to four front pockets. Women's has only two front pockets. Both have inside pocket as well. Available from Great Pacific Ironworks. $75.   **(Fig. 5-31)**

Tyrolean style jacket is knitted from 100% wool which is then boiled to produce a very tight, dense, water-repellent knit. Available from Country Store of Concorde. $140.

(Fig. 5-32)

LEATHER GARMENTS

The major leather animals are actually raised primarily for their meat, not for their hides. The hide is a by-product which in turn has its own by-products: The hair scraped from the skin is used to make plaster, hair felts, and rug pads; the excess flesh scraped from the skin is used as fertilizer, glue, and for the best quality gelatin.

Quality leather is hard to find and is expensive. Only a very small proportion of hides are perfect enough to be used for the best quality skins of smooth top grain with aniline finish; a slightly larger number are suitable for smooth leather with a pigment finish that will cover up minor blemishes; and the great majority must be embossed, buffed, sueded, or otherwise corrected in order to be used for garments.

In addition to its beautiful appearance, feel, and smell, leather has some very practical and remarkable properties. Leather's fibrous strands are built up of millions of coil-springlike protein molecules. These strands are twisted together into bundles and the bundles are also intricately entwined. This complex fiber network forms an untold number of interlocks within the skin which gives leather its very high tensile strength.

For the same reason, it has excellent tear resistance. Because the fibers are arranged randomly and not oriented in any particular direction, as they are in fabrics, there is no easy path for a rip to follow. Thus, leather edges do not need to be turned under and stitched to prevent raveling and tearing, and buttonholes, punch holes, and slits frequently do not need to be reinforced by stitching around the hole.

Leather can also flex freely in all directions thousands of times without damage. Its ability to stretch can be modified in the tanning process, from the needs of a glove to be very stretchy, to shoes that must stretch somewhat during the break-in period, to belting leather that should have minimum stretch. It can also be molded into a particular shape and maintain that shape indefinitely.

Thick hides are commonly split into layers of a usable thickness. The first, or hair side layer, is called "top grain" or "full grain" and has the typical animal grain. This part of the hide is the strongest and most durable. It takes the best finish and, if properly cared for, will wear for many years, becoming lustrous and richly patinaed with age. Top grain is the only layer that can be labeled "genuine leather."

Splits other than the top grain have a looser, more porous structure. They do not take as smooth a finish and tend to rough up during wearing. They are also less water-resistant. Most split leathers are given an embossed artificial grain finish, sometimes making them difficult to distinguish from genuine top grain.

Splits are often used to make sueded or napped leathers, which can also be made from top grain or full skins. When made from top grain or full leather, all the fibers on the flesh side (as opposed to the grain or hair side) of the skin are raised to a uniform height. If a piece of leather is sueded on both sides, it is probably a split.

Leather varies greatly in quality, not only from skin to skin and from top grain to split, but also according to which part of the animal it comes from. The center back sections of most animals produce the best leather because this part of the hide had to protect the animal against snow, rain, wind, and sun, and also against predators and brush. This section is known as the "bend." Leather from the belly and legs will be spongier, softer, and looser in texture. Animals that crawl instead of walk, however, such as alligator, lizard, and snake, develop fine belly section leathers.

TANNING

The Eskimos have traditionally clothed themselves in skins for warmth. But these were truly disposable garments—the skin, left in its natural, unpreserved state, soon began to decay and putrefy, and after a while the Eskimo would have to go out and catch another suit of clothes.

The purpose of tanning is to preserve the skin and to reflect the properties of the skin as it was when on the living animal. Skins go through many processes to become leather and each of these steps must be precisely regulated. A well-tanned skin will be supple and, with care, will last many years. Poorly tanned leather is stiff, short-lived, and feels more like cardboard.

Leather may be either vegetable tanned (also known as oak tanned) or mineral tanned. Vegetable tanning is one of the oldest methods known and originally employed oak bark ("tan" comes from "tannum," the Latin word for oak bark). Nowadays, the necessary tannic acid comes from many sources. The hides must be soaked in a solution of tannic acid for anywhere from two weeks to six months. Vegetable tanning can be identified by the characteristic tan color of the leather as you look along a cut edge. It makes a tough, sturdy leather that is frequently used for shoe soles. Vegetable-tanned leathers are more expensive because the process is so slow.

Chrome tanning, a form of mineral tannage that employs chromium salts, now constitutes about 85 percent of all tanning in this country. It can be identified along a cut edge by its typical light bluish-green color. It is a much faster process, taking only a few days, and makes a lighter, less dense leather that accepts a finish more readily. Chrome-tanned leather will last even longer than vegetable tanned. It is, however, somewhat more slippery when wet and less moisture resistant.

In combination tanning, the skin is tanned by one method and then retanned by a second, to combine the favorable characteristics of both. Oil-tanned leathers have generally been chrome tanned first and then heavily impregnated with oil to produce a very soft, supple leather. Fish oils, especially cod oil, are commonly used.

Pure oil tannage, characterized by a soft, yellow-colored leather, is used for chamois skins and some doe- and buckskin. A solution of cod or similar oil is kneaded in until a chemical reaction takes place that changes the skin into leather. Because the pores are particularly pronounced in oil tannage, large quantities of water can be absorbed. Chamois cloth continues to absorb water even when wet and will dry supple and undamaged. In the old days, pilots used to carry chamois skins in order to strain the gas that was stored in uncovered outdoor tanks; the chamois skin would absorb any water in the fuel.

The final stages of tanning are fat liquoring and finishing. Fat liquoring replaces the animal's fats removed during the tanning process; if this lubricating oil were not replaced, the leather would quickly dry out and crack. The fat liquoring process is very important in determining the suppleness and long life of the leather.

The leather is then dyed and finished. In dip dying or drum dying, the leather is fully immersed in dye and the color penetrates deeply. Spray dying spray-coats only one surface of the leather. This thin layer of coloring can wear off with use and, if nicked or scratched, the undyed leather beneath will be exposed. Spray dying also does not stand up well under commercial leather cleaning. Aniline dyes are transparent colors that can be used on only a small number of finest top grain skins because any blemishes on the leather will show clearly through the dye. Aniline dyes give leather a rich, mellow look. Opaque pigment dyes cover up minor blemishes and partially obscure the grain. Different types of leathers have special characteristics making them particularly appropriate for certain end-uses.

LEATHER TYPES

Calfskins and Cowhides

In America, the majority of leathers are obtained from cattle as a by-product of the meat-packing industry. However, the number of head slaughtered each year has recently been declining, quality cattlehides are becoming scarcer, and the price is rising accordingly. Also, there is a heavy foreign demand for American leather.

Calfskin, which is rarely available now, produces a smooth-surfaced, fine-grained, firm leather. It is durable, does not scuff easily, stretches only moderately, and takes a lustrous polish.

Cowhide has a more distinct grain and makes a durable, pliable leather.

Rawhide is not conventionally tanned but is instead treated with oils to preserve it. It is particularly tough but must be kept dry or it may rot and mildew. Rawhide will also shrink substantially if it gets wet.

Sheepskins and Lambskins

This is the second most used leather in America and comes from both imported and domestic sheep. Shearlings and sheepskins are tanned with the wool left on. Shearling is the hide of a young sheep that has been sheared no more than once. It produces a lightweight and supple garment leather. Sheepskin, on the other hand, is from an older sheep and tends to produce a heavier and stiffer hide. Electrified shearling or sheepskin, known as mouton, has a fine, velvety textured wool pile produced by chemically straightening the hair.

Cabretta is supple, very durable and, because of its tight grain, has good water repellency. It does not crack or peel. Cabretta is a medium-weight skin that cannot be split because it will lose its strength.

Capeskin comes from a hair sheep from South Africa, near Capetown. It is given a glazed finish.

Bench leather is a glazed lambskin.

Chamois cloth, originally from the chamois goat, is now made from a split of sheepskin that has been oil-tanned. It is impervious to water damage and will dry soft and supple.

Goatskin and Kidskin

Both these leathers are imported. Young kid or goat has a thin but strong, smooth skin with tiny holes on the grain side. As the animal matures, these markings become more pronounced.

Kidskin is porous and therefore particularly comfortable in shoes and gloves. It wrinkles easily. Kidskin takes a high glaze but, because of its thinness and softness, smooth kid-glazed leathers require careful handling to prevent scratching and peeling. Kid suede is a strong, durable leather.

Morocco leather is a vegetable tanned goatskin with a fine pebbly surface.

Deer, Doe, and Elk

These make porous, smooth-textured leathers with a good deal of stretch. Doeskin has an unusually soft luxurious feel. Because these are wild animals, their skins are usually scarred. Cowhide is often tanned to look like elk and is then referred to as elk-tanned leather.

Pigskin

Pigskin comes from the domesticated pig and from the peccary or wild hog. Peccary, which is becoming extremely rare, yields the best quality leather. Caution: Some wise guys here and there are peddling pig as genuine peccary.

All pigskin is identified by its markings of holes grouped in threes, caused by the removal of the bristles. These holes go right through the skin and serve not only as attractive markings but also as ventilation. It is a durable, soft, lightweight though rather stretchy leather, highly resistant to perspiration and moisture and, when wetted, will dry soft and stay soft.

The pig hide has always been difficult to remove from the animal without ruining the hide, but new methods are being developed and, with the price of cowhide going up, pigskin is likely to become increasingly popular.

Horsehide

Horsehide is an extremely tough, durable, scuff-resistant leather which is rarely available any longer.

Shell cordovan is not really leather but a cartilaginous layer from beneath the hide of the horse's hindquarters. It is extremely tough, nonporous, and makes very durable belts and shoes. It is uncommon today.

Furs

Furs are for us essentially luxury items. Expensive, delicate, and hard to care for, their practical aspects of warmth can be far better met by many other materials. Quality can vary greatly and the tanning process is difficult to ensure the fur is not damaged. Cost is largely dependent on which furs are in fashion; supply and demand and the amount of workmanship involved make up the balance of the price.

Furs must be protected from abrasion, so avoid sitting on them. They should be stored in a dry, cool place, on a broad-shouldered hanger. Allow plenty of room between garments. Never store in a plastic bag. Shake rather than brush to clean and, between seasons, place in cold storage. Never dry-clean; send to a furrier for refurbishment.

LEATHER CARE

Well-constructed garments of good quality leather are increasingly difficult to locate. Leather clothing companies on which you can rely for consistent high quality are few and far between. One thing is certain—if you do manage to locate and buy a good quality leather garment, it's unquestionably in your interest to take excellent care of it because quality leather clothing will not only become more expensive but even more rare than it is today. The quality leather garment you buy today will probably soon become a modern-day collector's item.

Heat damages leather; rain is injurious to leather and exposing wet leather to heat is the worst thing you can do. Wet leather *always* should be allowed to air-dry at room temperature. Once nearly dry, recondition the leather (unless it's suede) with Lexol (see Shoe Care, p. 127).

Working up a sweat in your leather clothing is to be avoided. Obviously, some perspiration is always going to be transmitted to the leather but if you expect to perspire profusely, leave your leather on the sidelines.

Periodically, clean and condition smooth leathers using Lexol. Every once in a while, maybe once a year, the garment (except suedes) can be lightly conditioned with some pure neat's-foot oil (not neat's-foot oil compound) or mink oil. It is extremely important that you not allow the surface of the skin to become tacky with conditioner because this encourages the build-up and absorption of dirt into the hide. Any tackiness or excess conditioner should be wiped off with a clean cloth.

Caution: Lighter-colored skins may be darkened and/or blotched by even top quality leather conditioners. However, conditioning is unavoidable and the patina produced by conditioners and by general wear and oxidation is part of the intrinsic beauty of fine leather. If this bothers you, you're probably better off with the immutable consistency of Naugahyde.

If you have a suede garment with a smooth top grain reverse side, you can condition the leather on this smooth back side with Lexol and, once in a great while if necessary, with a little pure neat's-foot oil. One thing you can do to help minimize the soiling of suede is to spray the garment while it's still brand new with a stain- and water-protector especially formulated for suede. French Creek (see listings) offers a good one called Protector 16.

As far as leather garments go, *don't* use saddlesoap on them. It's been our experience that this is a risky and generally impractical cleaning method—a cloth dampened with Lexol works very well to both clean and condition.

Everything that we have ever sent to so-called leather dry-cleaning specialists has come back the worse for wear. Sending leathers to a regular dry cleaner is *disastrous*. Perhaps somewhere in this world there may be a really safe leather dry cleaner. But, actually, if leather is cared for properly (which is not terribly difficult to do), it can in our opinion go comfortably for its lifetime without ever being dry-cleaned. So why gamble?

Leather clothes should never be stored in plastic bags. Hang on a broad-shouldered, preferably padded, hanger and drape a cloth over the garment to keep off dust. It is strongly recommended that you never store a leather garment folded up—crease marks can become permanently set.

Care of Shearling

In our view, there is not much sense in buying low-quality shearling or sheepskin coats. Basically, they just won't last. Besides, they look so cheap. On the other hand, high-quality shearlings and sheepskins will, barring abusive treatment, remain serviceable for many years.

As we've previously stated, we recommend never dry cleaning your coat. Every now and then, wipe it off with a damp cloth inside and out. Again, part of the beauty of shearling and sheepskin is that it develops a patina. Desiring a perpetually pristine appearance is an extravagantly unrealistic wish.

Regular gentle brushing with a nonwire suede brush will prevent build-up of dust and dirt and will keep the nap raised. Frequently, dirt marks can be rubbed out gently with a clean pencil eraser. Bald patches and some stains can be removed or at least diminished by lightly sanding with very fine emery paper. Keep in mind that the high-quality, drum-dyed shearling and sheepskins are much more stain-, water- and wear-resistant. For added protection, use a stain and water protector especially formulated for suede, such as French Creek's Protector 16. It is best to spray these on while the coat is still brand new.

Use a broad-shouldered, preferably padded, hanger for your coat and never wrap it in plastic; drape a cloth over it to keep off dust. Do not store it folded up; this can cause permanent crease marks.

LEATHER COAT AND JACKET SOURCES

There seems to be little question that French Creek is one of the finest shearling coat makers in the United States—indeed, probably in the world. French Creek uses only shearling skins, not sheepskins. They begin by carefully selecting only the finest specimens that are specially tanned to provide maximum durability and lifespan. Although exceptionally durable, the skins are also very supple and are drum-dyed during the tanning process, rather than being sprayed with dye, which is a less desirable coloring technique.

Each shearling coat is the work of a single artisan and is signed by its maker. All seams are double sewn for durability; stress points are riveted for extra strength. Buttonholes are expertly bound in top grade nude calfskin.

Because French Creek has such confidence in its quality of workmanship, they guarantee every garment unconditionally. Also, because they expect their garments to have a long lifespan, French Creek also maintains repair services.

In addition to uncommonly high quality, French Creek, because it sells directly to the public and does all its own manufacturing, manages to maintain some of the best prices you'll find. That's not to say that excellence comes cheap. But there's no question that French Creek makes a sincere effort—and successfully—to offer top quality at a most fair and just price.

By any standards, a French Creek Coat represents a unique investment for anyone who takes pride in the clothing they own. Seven examples are shown here.

Poncho cape: one size fits all. Brass snaps down the sides can be left open to wear as a cape or snapped closed to make a poncho. $500. **(Fig. 5-33)**

Aspen vest: cut slightly longer in back for additional warmth. $200. **(Fig. 5-34)**

Chester County, men's and women's: double-breasted front with woven leather buttons and slash pockets; hidden button tab to close collar. Women's version is neatly waisted, with shawl collar. $600. **(Fig. 5-35)**

CPO, men's and women's: shirttail hem; pockets and cuffs double-sewn; brass rivets and snaps. $350. **(Fig. 5-36)**

Fig.5-33

Fig.5-34

Fig.5-35

Fig.5-36

Fig.5-37

Fig.5-38

Steamer coat: calfskin-trimmed collar and pockets; leather elbow patches. Buckled cuffs and epaulets. Raglan sleeve. Capacious pockets are calfskin lined. $600.

(Fig. 5-37)

Saddle jacket and skirt to wear as separates or as a warm winter suit. Jacket, $350. Skirt, $200.   **(Fig. 5-38)**

Men's Knockaround: heavy-duty two-way zipper that opens from top or bottom. Large riveted pockets. Also available with shearling integral hood. $360.   **(Fig. 5-39)**

Shearling lined "flight" jacket made of imported goatskin with sheared lambskin body lining. Quilted lining in sleeves; wool knit wristlets and waistband. Collar of genu-ine mouton. Unfortunately, not available in women's sizes. A good deal by today's standards. Available from L. L. Bean. $209.   **(Fig. 5-40)**

Soft sueded lambskin is specially treated to protect against water-spotting. Made by Corbin Ltd., this fully lined jacket is carefully tailored, largely by hand. All seams are finished, with bound buttonholes and carefully matched skins. Two inside pockets. Available from Norm Thompson. $260.   **(Fig. 5-41)**

The Country Jacket is a well-crafted cowhide jacket. Made in England, all edges and seams are rolled and lock-stitched. Definitely an attractive investment. Available from Norm Thompson. $150.   **(Fig. 5-42)**

Fig.5-39

Fig.5-40

Fig.5-41

Fig.5-42

Fig.5-43

Fig.5-44

Fig.5-45

Fig.5-46

Fig.5-47   Fig.5-48   Fig.5-49

Sueded lambskin shirt-jac of high-quality New Zealand skins specially treated to resist soiling. Fully satin lined. Vented side seams. Available from L. L. Bean. $150.

(Fig. 5-43)

Brushed pigskin jacket with raglan sleeves and a quilted lining. Available from Orvis. $155.　　(Fig. 5-44)

Sawyer makes men's and women's shearling coats. Over the years Sawyer has had a fantastic reputation but it has been bought out by a large company and the original founding staff that built its reputation has left. We have some concern that the company may be in the process of changing. Nevertheless, they are still well thought of at the present time and we trust and hope that Sawyer will not be tempted to compromise on the quality it is now known for. Available nationally and from Norm Thompson. $295–725.　　(Figs. 5-45, 46)

A number of people, particularly two former top men from Abercrombie and Fitch, referred us to Huc of Sweden. We've met with their American representative and examined the goods at close range. Huc lives up to its illustrious reputation. There is very little like it anywhere. Beautiful hides are expertly constructed into fine works of clothing. Only a fool would fail to appreciate and cherish a Huc of Sweden garment. You'll find Huc only in the more expensive shops, frequently under private label, although sometimes the Huc lining will reveal its origins. Otherwise, ask the salespeople. If they haven't at least heard of Huc, there's something definitely lacking somewhere. If you want excellent leather, Huc is for you.

Huc jacket, style Rick. $500.　　(Fig. 5-47)

Huc overcoat, style Pierre. $800.　　(Fig. 5-48)

Huc Windbreaker, style Derby. $450.　　(Fig. 5-49)

Fig.5-50

Fig.5-51

Willis & Geiger flight jacket. Howard Geiger was the man who made, among other superb leather flight clothing, the famous G-1 goatskin flight jacket for U.S. Navy pilots during World War II. Although he has long since ceased making them for the Navy, he continues to produce the finest version of the G-1 available in the United States and probably in the world. It is without doubt the best of its kind.

There are other companies producing so-called replicas of the G-1. They have very seductive sales copy in their catalogs but when you actually see their merchandise, it becomes obvious their claims are grossly overrated. None of them can even come close to Mr. Geiger's beautiful flight jacket.

Technically, the present-day Geiger flight jacket is slightly different from the original World War II model but, in terms of quality of workmanship and materials, it is the equal in every respect. The goatskin is the best you'll find; stitching is very precise. It has the original bi-swing back design, inside map pocket, and genuine mouton fur collar. Our only minor criticism is that instead of a brass zipper, the jacket now has a heavy-duty nylon coil zipper. The color of the leather is also slightly lighter than the original, and the knit cuffs and waistband pill.

Nevertheless, it is a superbly executed leather garment and well worth every penny. Take our word for it, there isn't a better jacket anywhere. How long Mr. Geiger will continue making this jacket is uncertain so if you want one, you'd be well-advised to act promptly. Mr. Geiger, we salute you.

Available from Dennis Connor, Dunhams of Maine, and Orvis, or contact: Willis & Geiger, Inc., 45 West 36 St., New York, N.Y. 10018 (212) 695-5020. $250.   **(Fig. 5-50)**

Split-S Aviation Company, specializing in leather flight clothing, was just recently bought by Mr. James Wegge of Flight Suits Ltd. So we expect great things from Split-S.

At this moment we're not sure what products they'll be offering. We do know, however, that Mr. Wegge will be carrying a very nice replica of the early issue Army Air Corps A2 flight jacket.

Like the original A2, this one is made of goatskin. Though not an identical copy of the original military issue jacket, it's a good piece of workmanship. The goatskin is high quality, and stitching is small and neat. Solid brass Talon zipper, knitted wristlets and waistband of 100% wool, so pilling is not a problem. Fully rayon lined. Snap-close patch pockets. Collar tips also snap down for neat appearance.

Definitely one of the nicest jackets of its kind we've seen in a long time. Available by mail order from Split-S. $150.   **(Fig.5-51)**

INSULATED GARMENTS

Insulation-filled garments were developed in an effort to obtain a high degree of warmth with a minimum amount of weight. Whether down- or fiberfilled, a properly constructed insulated garment is a rather sophisticated piece of clothing engineering. Here are the basic facts to help you choose which of the two types of insulating fills are best for you.

DOWN

Down has greatly increased in price over the past five years or so. Although a typical jacket only contains about 10 ounces of down, it takes more than two geese to produce this much down. About 80 percent of our down is imported and, for the past several years demand has easily been outstripping supply.

The most expensive single ingredient in a down garment is the down itself. But the great differences in price from one down jacket to the next is not always in direct relation to the quality of the down being used. With the current extreme popularity of down, many manufacturers, particularly fashion manufacturers, are using poor-quality down. These jackets, in terms of function, are generally not worth investing in. They will not keep you as warm; they will not last as long; they will not serve you nearly as well as the genuine article.

Full-length down coats are a fashion item and, from a dollars and cents point of view, they are in our opinion a completely impractical investment. In order for down to insulate effectively, it must be right next to and surrounding your body. Down hanging around your legs is of negligible value. When walking, your constant leg movement pumps cold air inside the coat, negating any possible good the down could do. If you feel you need that much protection, you would be much better off wearing a pair of down overpants with a down jacket.

Down, according to the Federal Trade Commission, is "the undercoating of water fowl, consisting of light, fluffy filaments growing out from one quill point but without any quill shaft." Chickens when hatched are covered with down but quickly lose it as they grow older. Waterfowl, however, retain their down permanently under their outer feathers to serve as insulation against the cold.

Down is the most efficient insulative material currently available for use in clothing. It can be used in thicknesses far greater than any other material because it is extremely lightweight and readily compressible yet highly resilient. You can easily flex your arm or bend over when wearing a 2-inch thick down jacket, yet the down will spring back to its full thickness or "loft" when pressure is removed. Down will conform to your body shape, thus eliminating cold air pockets between the coat and yourself. It also absorbs body

moisture and dispels it to the outside air. In addition, with reasonable care, high-quality down will last many years.

Down is imported from eastern Europe, Asia, and China, where the geese and ducks are raised primarily for their meat, the feathers and down being harvested as a by-product. Until recently, these fowl were raised to their full maturity and a market goose weighed 25 to 30 pounds. But in the past decade or so, consumers have preferred eating smaller geese and ducks, weighing only 10 to 15 pounds. Because the birds are no longer being raised to maturity, this has had the unfortunate result that the down clusters available on the market are smaller in size and somewhat less resilient. Nevertheless, down still remains the most efficient insulator known.

There is no difference in the insulating power of duck and goose down. The only difference there has ever been between the two is that a fully grown goose is larger than a duck and so produces a larger down pod or cluster. It used to take slightly less goose than duck down to fill a given garment so a goose down parka would be slightly lighter, a very important factor to backpackers, mountain climbers, and the like. Now that geese are no longer being raised to full maturity, however, any pod size difference, and therefore difference in weight, is marginal. Frequently, duck and goose down are blended together.

Color also is irrelevant to quality or function. The only advantage of white down is that, in a pale-colored shell, it won't show through the fabric, as might gray down.

Terms such as "Prime Northern," "super loft," "100% prime" are not recognized by the Federal Trade Commission, are not standardized from one company to the next, and are nothing but advertising hype. Down is harvested from birds that are domesticated—not from wild fowl roaming in the icy cold wilderness growing extra layers of down to keep warm.

Fill power (the capacity of a unit weight of material to fill a given volume) is a measure of down's ability to "loft." Naturally, the lower the loft, the greater amount of down that would be needed to achieve a given thickness or warmth. Conversely, the higher the loft, the less down that would be needed, and the lighter the weight of the garment. This means less to the street wearer than to the mountaineer, where every ounce is crucial.

However, loft is *not* by itself a determinant of overall down quality. It is possible to have a low lofting down whose useful lifespan would considerably outlast a high lofting down.

Unfortunately, right now, there is no way for the consumer to know the overall quality of a down. You must rely totally on the manufacturer's integrity and expertise, which is why buying from a reputable manufacturer with a good track record is so essential. In order to assess the quality of down correctly, you must have considerable experience as well as a properly outfitted testing lab. This situation at present is, in our opinion, a sorry state of affairs. We feel the down clothing industry should work to develop some kind of index or rating system that would provide the consumer with a reasonably accurate reading of the overall quality in a given garment.

Naturally, a high-quality down garment will generally be more expensive. Good down, with reasonable care, however, should last easily 10 years, as compared with 3 or 4 years for a lesser-quality down.

The shell fabric should of course last as long as the down. It makes little sense to have a high-quality down encased in a low-quality shell fabric. Sloppy workmanship on the outside of the jacket is a good indication that what's inside won't be much better. However, high-class exterior workmanship is no guarantee that the down inside is of comparable quality.

Shell fabrics must also be down-proof. The best down-proof fabric has a high thread count. Some down will work its way through any fabric but if you hit the jacket a few times and see a lot of dust, fiber, or down escaping, select another jacket. Fabrics with a low thread count must be resin-filled and calendered to prevent down leakage; the necessary chemicals, heat, and pressure weaken the fabric. In addition, the resin treatment is not permanent and after a period of time, down will begin to leak out.

Most shell fabrics are lightweight; a heavy fabric would put enough weight on the down to reduce its loft. The use of leather as a shell material, except in very small quantities such as to reinforce a pocket or cuff, is totally inappropriate. Their respective proper cleaning methods are completely different and, unless the down is in a removable liner, either the down or the leather will suffer in cleaning.

We have found that the very lightweight ripstop nylon and nylon taffeta are poor choices for street wear. These fabrics are designed for backpacking use, where their lightness is a valuable asset. But for street use, they are too thin for durability and the thread count is generally not high enough to prevent eventual leakage. A strong, medium-weight shell is a better bet.

Down Labeling

The Federal Trade Commission sets labeling standards for down, as it does for other clothing materials. It requires that in order for a product to be labeled "down" or "down-filled," it must contain no less than 80 percent down (this 80 percent being made up of 70 percent down clusters and 10 percent individual down fibers) and no more than 18 percent waterfowl feathers. The remaining 2 percent is allowance for residue.

Products that contain less than this 80 percent down must be labeled a "blend" of down and feathers, and the particular blend must be identified, for example, by 90/10 or 80/20. But 90/10 does not mean it contains 90 percent down! It means that it contains 90 percent of the FTC's

minimum requirements for down. So a 90/10 product is actually only 73 percent down.

Within recent times, there has been a scandalous amount of mislabeling, some of it intentional, some out of ignorance. Whatever the explanation, you, the unwitting consumer, get ripped off twice: once, by not getting the quality you were promised; and twice, by getting stiffed with the higher price of the better quality down you were promised but never received. So, be cautious.

Because it is effectively impossible for the consumer to judge the contents of a down jacket and whether or not it is correctly labeled, this is all the more reason to buy only from a reputable dealer.

Following are the FTC's down labeling guidelines:

Federal Trade Commission Guidelines
Down Fillings   Labels will read:

Content	Down	90/10	80/20	70/30	60/40
Minimum					
Down Clusters	**70%**	**63%**	**56%**	**49%**	**42%**
Maximum					
Down Fiber	10%	10%	10%	10%	10%
Maximum					
Feathers	**18%**	**25%**	**32%**	**39%**	**46%**
Maximum					
Residue	2%	2%	2%	2%	2%
	100%	100%	100%	100%	100%

(Above information from the F.T.C. "Guidelines for the Feather and Down Products Industry," 1971.)

Caring for Down

Down clothing must be cared for properly. Dirty down loses some of its loft and therefore will not insulate as well. A down garment should be cleaned once or maybe twice during the season, as necessary. In addition, periodically tossing it into the dryer on a low heat setting for a brief spin will increase its loft by electrostatically charging the down. (Remember, stains can be heat set, so be sure your garment is clean.)

Between seasons, store the garment loosely, never stuffed in a bag or jammed into a drawer. It should lie flat or be placed loosely in a box, rather than hung on a hanger. If you do use a hanger, be sure it is a broad one, not a skinny wire hanger. Never store it in a plastic bag because condensation can form inside the bag and lead to mildewing or actual rotting of the down.

Although it is desirable to air out your down clothes occasionally in the sun and air, direct hot sunlight can damage down if the sun is allowed to heat the surface of the garment for an extended period of time. The natural oils of the down close to the surface may be cooked away, thus destroying the individual down plumules and, as a result, decreasing loft.

Cleaning Down

There is a great deal of controversy within the down industry as to whether down can or cannot be safely dry cleaned. This argument could be resolved easily by conducting a simple test program on down to see how it responds to dry cleaning; whether indeed the cleaning solvents do, as alleged by many, strip the down of its natural oils, thereby embrittling it and severely shortening its lifespan.

Such a test could be performed easily by any well-established testing lab. However, neither down manufacturers nor any of the clothing industry associations seem sufficiently interested to pursue this and so the controversy, ignorance, and guessing games continue, and it is the consumer who suffers the most.

Our personal recommendation is that you wash your down garment yourself if at all possible. There are no arguments about home washing; the experts we interviewed unanimously agree that it is a safe method and many experts say it is the only safe method. All agree as well that it is important to do it the *right* way and carefully. Some manufacturers (who personally wash their own down garments) have told us that the only reason they publicly recommend dry cleaning over washing is because they are concerned that washing instructions may not be properly followed, the garment may be damaged, and they will be held responsible. Before blithely ignoring a DRYCLEAN ONLY label on a down garment, however, check with the manufacturer: there might be components in that particular garment that could be harmed by washing.

We strongly suspect another reason why the dry cleaning versus washing controversy has not been conclusively settled is because dry-cleanability is considered an important sales asset and many manufacturers would just prefer to assume that dry cleaning is safe.

Another major controversy is the question of what type of dry-cleaning solvent is best: perchloroethylene (perk) which is used by approximately 80 percent of the cleaners in this country, or the less common Stoddard fluid process. None of the numerous experts we questioned could provide any demonstrable evidence which clearly showed that one was better than the other. There was unanimous agreement though that a high-quality dry cleaner who specializes in the cleaning of down is imperative. CAUTION: *A down garment with a Gore-Tex shell cannot be dry cleaned;* it must be washed.

We know of two reputable down dry-cleaning specialists who will work by mail:

Down East
93 Spring Street
New York, N.Y. 10012
(212) 925-2632

The Down Depot
108A Carl Street
San Francisco, Cal. 94117
(415) 664-4313

Washing Down

The most basic advantage in washing down yourself is that you have control over all the stages of the process and know that your cleaning fluid (water) is clean, whereas the dry cleaner's may not be.

Use one of the concentrated free-rinsing soaps used by the down processors. We particularly like Nu-Down. Do not use detergent, which tends to strip the oils from the down and also can leave behind a residue that may cause matting and clumping. DO NOT USE BLEACH: This will seriously damage down, which is a proteinaceous substance, just like wool and silk.

Either hand or machine wash. Some people claim that the agitator vanes in a top loading machine place undue stress on the garment. This applies particularly in the case of sleeping bags which have very delicate interior baffles that can be ripped out fairly easily. Top loaders set on *gentle* cycle are generally safe for garments but if you have a choice, it would probably be better to use a front loading machine because that eliminates the chance of a freak accident occurring.

If your garment is particularly soiled in places, preclean these areas with a little soap and water. Then fill the washer with warm water, add the soap, and mix it well. It is advisable to first wipe out the tub with a damp paper towel to remove any dirt or soap scum. Then submerge and spread out your garment in the water so it is evenly distributed. *Run it on the gentle cycle.*

We always put our down clothing through the rinse cycle twice to be sure all the soap is removed because any soap residue left on the down will reduce its ability to loft.

When removing the garment from the water, lift it very carefully and *always* support its weight from underneath. Instead of being its normal dry weight of about 1½ pounds, a wet jacket will weigh about 30 pounds. This extra weight must be carefully supported or it could cause the stitching to rip out. After the spin cycle is over, your prized jacket will look like a scraggly drowned rat as you take it out of the washer. Believe us—don't be upset.

If you have access to a centrifugal extractor, place the garment in there, spreading it out evenly, and run it through a cycle or two to spin out additional water before putting it in the dryer.

If you do not have an extractor, place it in a bathtub or large sink and gently squeeze out the water. *Do not wring.* Actually, you should never wring out any garment but this holds particularly true for down. Next spread it out on a clean dry towel, roll it up, and press out more water.

Removing as much water as you can not only saves energy in the dryer but also saves additional unnecessary abrasion from the coat rubbing against the dryer drum, and reduces the risk of tumbling the heavy weight and thereby ripping out seams.

Use a low to medium heat setting on a home dryer. Commercial dryers use a higher heat and their thermostats are not always reliable so use *only a low setting* on these machines. Adding a couple of clean towels will help absorb additional moisture.

Down garments must be dried thoroughly. Not only will damp down mildew and rot, but if it is not thoroughly dried, the down will remain matted and clumped together, resulting in significantly less loft and therefore less warmth. It may take several hours to dry it fully. Check the drying progress periodically. Squeeze the garment; as long as you can still feel clumps of down, it is not yet dry enough.

Toward the middle part of drying, throw in a clean sneaker or better yet a couple of clean tennis balls. These will help break up remaining clumps and fluff up the down.

If you will not be wearing your jacket again immediately, or if you are putting it away for summer storage, it is a good idea to leave it out to air for a few days to let any lingering moisture evaporate before storing it.

A cleaned down garment should not only look clean but also have a greater loft because it is no longer weighed down by dirt and oils and the static electricity produced in the dryer also contributes to loft.

Synthetic Fiberfills

Synthetic fiberfills claim an advantage over down because they retain about half of their insulating capacity when wet, whereas down loses a lot more of its warmth. If you are just wearing a coat around town, this doesn't really matter all that much; you can always go home and change if you get caught in a downpour. But if you are going to be out boating or at a sporting event on a rainy day, it could indeed make a difference. Fiberfills do, though, absorb water far more readily than down, although they also dry out more quickly. It takes a good deal of exposure to water to saturate clean down.

Fiberfills are generally less expensive than down although the price difference is steadily decreasing. They are also heavier than down, averaging about one-third greater weight in a garment. Again, this is a distinction far more important for backpackers and climbers.

Perhaps the most substantial difference between down and fiberfills, in respect to normal everyday wear, is that high-quality down has a significantly longer lifespan than fiberfills. The generally accepted life expectancy for fiberfills, at least among the experts we consulted, is little more than five years, assuming reasonable care; this is because the crimp, which provides the loft, fatigues and eventually flattens out. On the other hand, for a high-quality down, the lifespan is about ten years plus, also assuming reasonable care. As a long-term investment, good-quality down can average out to be far *less* expensive than fiberfills.

If you will be working outdoors, however, exposing the coat to the elements and to conditions of sweating and soiling, fiberfills will maintain their loft better when wet. Also, a shell fabric, when subjected to heavy dirt and abrasion, is likely to wear out within the five-year lifespan of a fiberfill anyway, making the more expensive down jacket a possibly impractical investment for a work coat. (A down and feather blend, which is less expensive than down, might be worth considering.) You are likely to feel a little less comfortable in a fiberfill because these are somewhat bulkier and do not absorb perspiration as well as down.

The two most popular and highly regarded fiberfills are Hollofil and PolarGuard.

DuPont Hollofil II (which used to be called Fiberfill II) is a hollow, short-stranded filament, averaging 2½ inches in length, of Dacron polyester fiber. In theory, the hollow fibers create a filling mass with about 17 percent more volume than solid polyester fibers of the same weight. The fibers are specially coated to reduce fiber-to-fiber friction and thereby increase loft. Because Hollofil is manufactured in short strands, garments must be carefully constructed and quilted to keep the strands evenly distributed throughout the coat.

Celanese PolarGuard is a continuous filament polyester fiberfill with a heat- and resin-set crimp. This continuous filament batting provides superior strength and lasting loft. It is also less prone to shifting and requires less quilting because of its continuous filament design. It can therefore tolerate a more poorly constructed garment than can Hollofil.

PolarGuard was approved by the military as a replacement for down about five years ago. One of the primary reasons for seeking a down substitute is down's relative scarcity and the fact that most of it is imported.

We have found in our research that PolarGuard is frequently preferred over Hollofil by serious, technically minded outdoor people.

Cleaning Synthetic Fills

Synthetic fill garments should be treated with the same care as down garments. They must never be dry cleaned, however, because some solvents remove the fiber coatings and reduce or destroy the ability of the fill to loft.

Washing instructions are much the same as for down, with a few special considerations.

Synthetic fiberfills are thermoplastics, so they can be easily damaged by heat. In manufacture, the individual fibers are heat-set "crimped" to contribute to loft. If these fibers are overheated, they begin to lose their crimp and hence their loft. Washing and drying temperatures must therefore be carefully regulated. Also, avoid storing garments in hot places—by a radiator or steam pipe, in the trunk of your car, or in an attic during the summer, for example.

When washing, check the water temperature with your hand. If it is too hot for your hand, it is too hot for fiberfill. Use a mild detergent rather than a soap.

Proceed as with the down washing instructions and dry on a *low* setting.

THINSULATE

Thinsulate, within certain limits, contradicts the general rule that all textile materials of equal thickness will, for all practical purposes, be of equal warmth. Thinsulate can provide approximately half again as much warmth for thickness of any other garment material.

However, Thinsulate cannot be used in thicknesses much greater than 1/2 inch, without becoming too heavy and bulky for comfort. This 1/2-inch thickness would provide the equivalent warmth of approximately a 3/4-inch thick down or fiberfill jacket and would weigh considerably more. But, because down and fiberfill jackets are generally considerably more than 3/4-inch thick, a conventional (1/2-inch thick) Thinsulate jacket will be *less warm than* a conventional (2-inch thick) down or fiberfill jacket.

So don't let anyone tell you, as some have tried to tell us, that a Thinsulate jacket is warmer than a down jacket. In a laboratory comparison of the two materials, Thinsulate is technically warmer, but you have to compare the materials as they are actually used in a jacket to come up with a fair and truthful reading.

In addition, Thinsulate is made predominately of olefin fibers with some polyester added for strength. Olefin is well known for its extremely poor resilience, which means that Thinsulate would be likely to crush down easily, reducing its loft and therefore severely reducing its insulative value and life expectancy.

Thinsulate cannot be dry cleaned; it must be washed. And because olefin melts at a low temperature, very cool washing and drying temperatures must be used. It has not been on the market long enough to determine its longevity but olefin is notorious for its poor durability. In addition, Thinsulate is expensive.

Thinsulate is an interesting step in the continuing search for a more efficient insulative material but it is far from being the wonder material that it is touted as in some quarters.

INSULATED GARMENTS: GENERAL GUIDELINES

Not all insulated garments are constructed alike. Garments filled with down or other insulation must be quilted in order to keep the insulation evenly distributed around you, but there are various ways to quilt. PolarGuard is an exception in that it can be but does not have to be quilted at all. Because it is a continuous filament batting, no other stitching is needed if it is held securely at the seams. Nevertheless, manufacturers using PolarGuard frequently quilt it anyway because it gives the "look" they think the public likes.

Quilting Methods

Sewn-through construction, where the down or fiberfill is quilted between two layers of lightweight shell fabric, is the simplest to fabricate. This makes a very light and compressible garment, but cold can penetrate at the quilt lines where there is no insulation. The exposed quilt stitching is also susceptible to snagging and breaking.

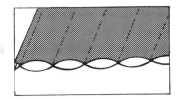

Down construction—sewn through

Adding a fabric layer over the sewn-through layer eliminates cold spots along quilting lines and traps additional dead air space for insulation. The unquilted outer shell also protects the quilting stitches against abrasion or snagging. This triple-layer construction makes a slightly heavier but also warmer and more durable garment.

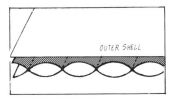

Down construction—extra layer

Offset baffle construction maximizes warmth with two sewn-through layers positioned so that each line of quilting is covered by the other layer's pocket of down. This construction can also be used with a separate outer shell for heavy-duty warmth. There is no question that this is a superior design but, except in the harshest of climates, the improved warmth this type of construction offers is probably unnecessary for normal streetwear. In addition, it's an awful nuisance to repair.

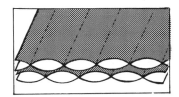

Down construction—offset baffle

Quilting lines generally run horizontally; when they are sewn vertically, all the down will work its way to the bottom of the jacket, leaving you with a warm waist and a cold torso. Horizontal quilting keeps the down evenly distributed and held in place.

An important word on fit: Insulated clothing should not fit snugly. A parka that is too small will constrict and compress the down or fiberfill, reducing its insulative value. A parka should fit just loose enough so as not to compress the insulation. If you fall in between sizes, we feel it is always better to opt for the slightly larger size. Also, remember to allow room for a bulky sweater or insulated vest. And if you want to be able to wear a sports jacket underneath, be sure the coat is long enough to cover it—many of them are several inches too short.

Raglan sleeves eliminate shoulder-top seams that might collect rain or snow or create cold spots. The body should be long enough to cover your rump—this is the preferred length for warmth.

On insulated jackets, look for a high neck with snaps or Velcro closure to keep out cold drafts and substitute for a scarf. However, too many layers around the neck can become bulky and uncomfortable. If you plan to wear an insulated vest underneath regularly, choose a vest with a scoop neck or stretch-knit collar, rather than a stand-up collar.

Two-way zippers give you more control over ventilation—you can unzip from either the top and/or the bottom. Also, when you sit down, you can unzip from the bottom and release strain on the zipper without having to open the coat completely. Zipper tape should be inserted *between* the inner and outer fabric for greatest strength. A less satisfactory alternative is for the zipper tape to be double-stitched with two rows of stitching. Delrin plastic tooth zippers have an excellent reputation; coil zippers cause less damage to fabric that becomes caught in the zipper. Coil zippers, however, especially the lightweight ones, tend to have a higher failure rate than high-quality tooth zippers. Zipper pulls should be large enough so you can get a comfortable grip on them, especially when wearing gloves.

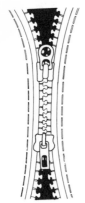

Two-way zipper

A storm flap over the zipper with either snaps or Velcro closure gives double protection against wind and cold and also provides a back-up system should the zipper break. Check the quality of the snaps and whether they open easily but also close securely.

Drawcords at waist, hem, and hood seal cold air out and warm air in. Rather than tying the waist cord in front of you,

simply knot off each end as shown. Storm skirts provide the same service.

Drawcord at waist of jacket

Storm skirt on jacket

To prevent cold air blowing up cuffs and warm air seeping out, look for knitted wristlets, snap closures, or Velcro tape, which offers the greatest versatility.

Hoods are always a valuable asset on insulated jackets. If you have the option of buying a separate hood, take it. On mountain shells, hoods are a very important and very tricky part of the garment. For one thing, your head tends to turn *inside* the hood, without the hood turning along with you. So, on a poorly designed hood, you end up looking into the hood and lose your peripheral vision. Drawcords that hold the hood snugly to your head help in this regard. A stiffened bill is also very important to keep the rain off your face and out of your eyes, especially if you wear glasses.

Pockets

Cargo pockets should be bellows or box style to allow ample expansion. When trying on the jacket or shell, zip it closed and stuff your hands into the pockets. If this is hard to do, reject it. Handwarmer pockets, behind cargo pockets, are often insulated on insulated jackets.

Vertical breast pockets should zip closed downward to prevent accidental opening.

Slash breast pockets are a rarely seen, but excellent feature for keeping hands warm. Especially good for walking in the rain, because rain will not drip down your sleeve straight into your pocket.

Back pockets provide extra cargo space.

Pocket closures: Zippers make a secure closure but can be difficult to operate when hands are cold or gloved.

Snaps or Velcro are easier to use with gloves but, because they do not fully close the whole pocket opening, are less secure. A doubled-over pocket top combined with snaps or Velcro is the best method, as safe as a zipper and easy to handle with gloves or cold hands. Also, it provides the best protection against rain, dirt, and snow infiltration.

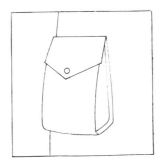

Cargo pocket, box style

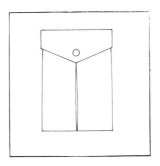

Cargo pocket, bellows style

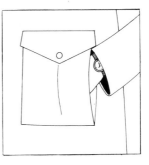

Hand-warmer pocket

Back pocket

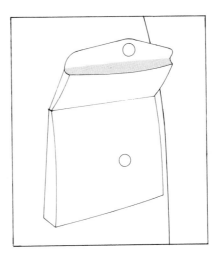

Doubled-over pocket top

Fig.5-52

Fig.5-53   Fig.5-54

INSULATED GARMENT SOURCES

We called all over the country for opinions on the best down and insulated clothing companies. The name Camp 7 was repeatedly recommended to us by mountaineers. Their down has a very good reputation and inspection of their garments' workmanship clearly indicates a serious concern for quality. The three examples shown are all available from Camp 7.

Down Pamir: polyester/cotton shell. $125.   **(Fig. 5-52)**

Down Cascade: choice of taffeta or polyester/cotton shell. $109.   **(Fig. 5-53)**

Down vest has no sewn-through shoulder seams; extra long back. Taffeta or polyester/cotton shell. Taffeta, $60. Polyester/cotton, $64.   **(Fig. 5-54)**

We've heard good reports about Banana Equipment, particularly their 100% nylon pile. It's supposed to have good pill resistance. Available from Holubar.   **(Fig. 5-55)**

Canor Plarex/Helly-Hansen is another producer of fiber-pile garments with an excellent reputation. Available nationally.

Time and again, Marmot Mountain Works has been recommended to us as one of the best and most innovative companies of its kind. This isn't to say that they're by any means infallible but, judging from the equipment we've seen and the reports we've heard, they have all the earmarks of a serious clothing company.

Marmot has a lot of confidence in Gore-Tex (discussed on page 106 and is using it not only in their parkas but in the shells of some of their down jackets as well. Neither of us is sold on the true practicality of Gore-Tex, at least for normal wear. We know many experts still share our doubts.

Nevertheless, Marmot's design and attention to detail have to be given very serious consideration. They use some of the highest fill power down available on the American market. The four examples shown are available from Marmot Mountain Works.

Fig.5-55

Fig.5-56

Marmot has a variety of excellent down parkas for different comfort ranges, all of them available with either a tightly woven nylon or a Gore-Tex shell. All shell fabrics are individually hot-cut to prevent frayed seams and each garment is sewn entirely by one person. This is their mid-range model for men and women called the Warm II. $128.

(Fig. 5-56)

This is the lighter weight, neatly fitting New Warm I. Intelligent shoulder and arm design provides great freedom of movement. Knitted cuffs and storm skirt keep out cold. Gore-Tex only. $159.

(Fig. 5-57)

Fig.5-57

Fig. 5-58

Marmot down vest with down-filled hand-warmer pockets, down-filled storm flap behind zipper. Velcro neck closure. Cut 2″ longer in back for additional protection. $73. **(Fig. 5-58)**

Marmot 100% nylon fiber pile fleece. $40. **(Fig. 5-59)**

Fig. 5-59

Fig.5-60

Trailwise has been repeatedly complimented by the out-door experts we've questioned. We have several of their down garments and have been very pleased with them. Shown here is the Logan in 65/35 cloth, an intimate blend of polyester and cotton. Available from The Ski Hut. Men's, $115. Women's $108.   **(Fig. 5-60)**

Northface is another dependable insulated clothing source. Their down vest with 65/35 shell is pictured here. In addition to the four external pockets there is also an inner pocket. Available from Northface. $60.   **(Fig. 5-61)**

Fig.5-61

Fig.5-62

Fig.5-63

Eddie Bauer is one of the oldest and best-respected American names in down clothing. We've had a good deal of experience with Bauer products and have always been very satisfied. Their customer service and return policies are exemplary. Bauer has a well-developed product testing program; we do feel, given this fact and their leadership role in the industry, that Bauer should consider providing more technical information on their down content. Seven of their classics are shown. Available from Eddie Bauer.

The Downlight Canadian. We've had ours for eight years now and they've proven to be an exceedingly practical investment. Great for traveling or as an extra layer of warmth under a raincoat or even a down jacket. $40.   **(Fig. 5-62)**

The Weskit is similar to the Downlight Canadian but designed to fit trimly under a sports or suit jacket. $30.

(Fig. 5-63)

The Northwesterner is serviceable and handsome. Durable blend of polyester and cotton outer fabric. Copious mouton collar conceals down-insulated foul weather hood. Two-way front zipper under buttoned storm flap. Stretch knit nylon wristlets. $180.   **(Fig. 5-64)**

Fig.5-64

Another Bauer classic is their All-Purpose jacket. Outer fabric is a durable blend of nylon and cotton, with ripstop nylon lining. Slash pockets are lined with nylon fleece. $85.   **(Fig. 5-65)**

The Superior Polar Parka has been imitated but, as far as we know, never surpassed. Bauer claims its comfort range is good for -70° F. Outer fabric is a tough nylon and cotton blend. Protective hood ruff of coyote fur. Tunnel drawcords at waist and hem. Sleeves have stretch knit nylon wristlets. In addition to four outer pockets, there are two large inside pockets as well. Heavy-duty two-way brass zipper. $325.   **(Fig. 5-66)**

Women's stadium coat with outer shell of polyester and cotton, has mouton lamb collar. $160.   **(Fig. 5-67)**

Men's Northwind. Outer shell is tough nylon/cotton blend; inner fabric is polyester and cotton. Tunnel drawcord at waist; stretch knit nylon wristlets. Heavy-duty zipper under button-down storm flap. Available with either cloth or mouton collar. A rugged, lightweight coat, good, according to Bauer, to −40°F. $140.   **(Fig. 5-68)**

Fig. 5-65

Fig. 5-66

Fig.5-67

In New York City, in the heart of the Soho district, resides a most interesting and talented fellow, one Leon Greenman. Leon is a seasoned outdoor and mountain climbing veteran and is widely credited with inventing the term *backpacking*.

He now owns and operates a unique store called Down East. He repairs and services all types of down and fiberfill clothing, as well as most other kinds of outdoor equipment, including boots. Customizing and modifications are also big parts of Leon's repertoire. If you have a down parka to which you want to add some special feature, Leon's the person to consult. He also makes packs and various kinds of bags and satchels; sells fabrics and heavy-duty zippers; books, maps, and a range of other paraphernalia that are difficult to find elsewhere.

There may be others but Leon is the only expert we know of who has the skill and patience to repair insulated clothing properly. From our own experience, we know him to be a very conscientious and fair-minded person. We certainly feel safe entrusting any of our prized garments to his capable hands.

You can mail him your garments for servicing and repair. He also will dry clean down clothing by mail. Write a letter carefully explaining what you want done. If you call him in advance, Leon will even arrange to have UPS pick up your package and return it to you COD.

Down East, 93 Spring Street, New York, N.Y. 10012 (212) 925-2632. Phones attended after 12 noon.

Fig.5-68

RAINGEAR

In many situations, rain can be coped with by using an umbrella, pulling your jacket over your head, or scurrying for the nearest shelter. But when rain is heavy and you must be out in it, have some consideration for your clothes.

Most conventional shoes and boots can be severely damaged by rain and snow. Some of the harm can be averted if you promptly stuff them with paper, anoint them with Lexol, and allow them to dry at room temperature (see p. 127 for further details). But if you get them wet on your way to work, then you may have to wear them all day and be unable to take care of them. So either wear rubber overboots or keep a special pair of shoes for rain that also look good enough to wear as you go about your daily work.

Pants also should be chosen with some thought for the rain. For example, a durable tight-weave fabric is a good choice. Filsons are excellent because they will not easily wrinkle and will keep a sharp crease through inclement conditions.

Raingear does tend to be rather a problem. Water-repellent materials won't keep you dry for long in a heavy rain; waterproof fabrics will keep you dry but tend to make you hot and damp because they don't let your body moisture out. A poncho of waterproof material is a good solution because it allows sufficient ventilation to keep you dry and comfortable inside while protecting you against the rain. The U.S. Army makes an excellent lightweight, urethane-coated, ripstop nylon poncho with a good hood design. It's available only in olive drab.

For short journeys into light rain, a raincoat of tightly woven cotton or a fabric treated with a water-repellent finish such as Zepel or Scotchgard is fine, as is a tightly knitted oiled wool sweater.

Bear in mind that water repellent finishes serve little use unless the fabric is woven tightly enough to prevent the passage of water droplets. These finishes are not permanent and need to be reapplied periodically.

A few special cotton fabrics, such as Ventile cloth, are so tightly woven that they require no water-repellent finish. When dampened by rain, the yarns of their extra tight weave swell, blocking the entry of water. Thomas Black and Sons is the only company we know of offering garments made of Ventile. For a local source, inquire: P.O. Box C.P. 4501, Ottawa, Ontario, K1S 5H1 (613) 235-1461.

For longer forays, you need waterproof gear. The basic choices are PVC, polyurethane, rubber, and Gore-Tex. Gore-Tex is discussed later. The advantage of urethane is that, because it is so strong, it can be coated onto a very thin fabric, making it a light yet waterproof garment. Unfortunately, PVC, urethane, and rubber all come in varying grades of quality and there is no way to tell one grade from another when you're buying. Although the basic ingredients are the same for all grades, the special additives that can protect against degradation from ozone, ultraviolet light, pollutants, and that prevent hardening and cracking in the cold, vary greatly from one grade to the next. A reputable manufacturer is your only safeguard in buying.

Construction is also very important. Even if the material is impermeable, rain can often leak in through the seams. A flat-felled seam is preferable to a plain seam, but flat-felled seams must face *down* to shed rain. In addition, they should be sealed.

Welded seams are the best; in these, the pieces of material being joined have actually been fused together so no rain can penetrate. Other sealing methods are to bond a piece of tape over the seam on the inside or to run a line of liquid sealer that congeals when dry over the inside of the seam.

GORE-TEX

Over the years, both the military and private industry have spent millions of dollars in search of a breathable, waterproof material, one that will prevent any rain from penetrating yet that will at the same time allow body moisture to escape so the wearer doesn't become sweat-soaked. Thus it must combine the seemingly contradictory properties of being impermeable to liquid water yet permeable to moisture vapor (sweat). In other words, it must be both porous and nonporous.

There have been many products which have come and gone that claimed to have solved this difficult and challenging engineering feat. A recent and widely heralded new product in this area is Gore-Tex, manufactured by W. L. Gore Associates in Elkton, Md.

Gore-Tex is an expanded polytetrafluorethylene film which has about 9 billion pores to the square inch. Because each pore is 20,000 times smaller than a drop of water, liquid water cannot penetrate readily. Yet each pore is 700 times larger than a molecule of water *vapor* and therefore vapor from the body can readily escape through the film.

This film is then laminated to a porous shell fabric such as a taffeta or ripstop nylon. Gore-Tex is also available in a three-layer laminate, where the film is sandwiched between the outer shell fabric and a thin knitted inner fabric which protects the film against abrasion. This laminate will feel somewhat stiffer and heavier than the two-layer type.

When you buy a Gore-Tex jacket, you must seal the seams yourself if the garment is to be watertight in heavy rain. This is a messy and a time-consuming job that must be done very carefully and be repeated periodically.

Gore-Tex works in theory; in the field, expert users have been running into some problems.

The most common problem is leakage—not through the seams if these have been properly sealed, but through the fabric itself. Apparently, contamination of the film with oils, whether from the body, oiled wool sweaters, cooking oils, some insect repellents, and tanning lotions, can reduce the surface tension of the film, thereby permitting leakage.

Some testers feel that even the presence of dust or dirt will cause leaks. This problem can generally be corrected once the garment is washed but it must be kept meticulously clean at all times. If leakage persists after laundering, washing the garment in denatured alcohol should restore waterproofness. Gore-Tex must never be dry cleaned.

Another major problem is delamination. We have seen a large bag of Gore-Tex garments in a camping store waiting to be returned to the garment manufacturers because the film had delaminated. (This was not the garment manufacturers' fault—Gore-Tex is sold prelaminated.) W. L. Gore, however, has reportedly now remedied this particular problem.

Altogether, there are very mixed feelings about the effectiveness of Gore-Tex. It is also quite expensive and the price continues to rise.

Two new breathable waterproof fabrics are coming on the market soon and a good friend of ours, who is a clothing evaluation engineer, tells us that his test results show they are better than Gore-Tex. In fact one of them, being made by Reeves Bros., is apparently substantially superior to Gore-Tex.

All this just shows that the quest for a breathable waterproof material is far from over and one must exercise considerable caution before investing.

MOUNTAIN SHELLS

Mountain shells are designed to be worn over an insulated jacket to keep the jacket dry and to reduce wind chill in inclement weather. Buy a size large enough to be worn over your jacket without compressing the down and be sure it is long enough to cover the bottom of the jacket. It will also provide substantially more warmth on very cold or windy days.

Surprising as it may sound, a mountain shell can also be worn alone in the rain and, even though it is oversize, it is cut so that it still fits well over just a light sweater. We always put ours to this dual use.

For specifics on particular features to look for, refer to the insulated garment section.

RAINGEAR SOURCES

Sierra Designs has been around for a long while and continues to be one of the better quality suppliers of down clothing and other outdoor gear. Their 60/40 parka shown here is a classic and is constantly imitated by other companies. We each have one and have found it in general to be a very good garment. The fact that it has a single instead of two-way zipper is a liability in our minds and the neck windflap is a bit of a problem because it sometimes gets caught in the zipper. Also, it significantly loses its water-repellency after the first cleaning. Otherwise, it's an admirable piece of work. Available from Sierra Designs. $105. **(Fig. 5-69)**

Fig.5-69

Fig.5-70

Fig.5-71

Fig.5-72

Fig.5-73

Fig.5-74

Marmot Mountain Works Night Rider cycle jacket provides excellent night-time protection; Early Warning, a special newly developed reflective finish by 3M produces exceptionally high visibility. Illustration shows a conventional blaze orange nylon Windbreaker next to the Early Warning jacket, which appears bright white, although it is actually a dark blue. Available from Marmot Mountain Works. $100. **Fig. 5-70)**

Camp 7's Trail Ridge: available in either Gore-Tex or 9 oz. cotton duck, both lined with nylon taffeta. Coil zipper. No sewn-through shoulder seams. Front zippered pockets; inner back pocket. Waist drawcord. Extra long sleeves. Available from Camp 7. Duck, $59. **(Fig. 5-71)**

Genuine U.S. military urethane-coated ripstop nylon poncho. Absolutely one of the best ponchos made anywhere—we each have one. All seams coated and sealed. Lightweight, folds up compactly. Particularly well-suited for hot weather rain protection. Available from Brigade Quartermaster. $19. **(Fig. 5-72)**

Line 7 is highly respected for its foul weather gear. Manufactured of PVC coated nylon, with seams both stitched and welded. Available at marine stores, or for a local source, inquire: Line 7, Inc., P.O. Box 3114, Annapolis, Md. 21403 (301) 268-8182. Jacket, $99. Pants, $75. **(Fig. 5-73)**

Henri-Lloyd is another famous name in marine clothing. The consort jacket pictured here is an all-purpose quilt-lined jacket with heavy-duty nylon zipper and button storm flap. Velcro closure pockets, adjustable storm cuffs. All seams are machine sewn, then hand taped for 100% waterproofness. Quilted detachable hood is optional. Jacket is also available unlined.

The Consort flotation jacket (not shown) is lined with close-celled foam for those of you who might tend to go overboard. Available at marine stores, or for a local source, inquire: Bacon and Assoc., P.O. Box 3150, Annapolis, Md. 21403 (301) 263-4880. Consort jacket, $110. Flotation jacket, $210. **(Fig. 5-74)**

Fig.5-75

Canor Plarex/Helly-Hansen makes very high-quality waterproof marine wear and industrial clothing. Made of PVC (polyvinyl) coated to high-quality long staple cotton. All seams are electronically welded for total waterproofness. Available at marine stores, or for a local source, inquire: Canor Plarex, Inc., 4200 Twenty-third Ave W., Seattle, Wash. 98199 (206) 283-0133. Jacket, $57, Pants, $28.
(Fig. 5-75)

Peter Storm makes a very good line of foul weather gear. They offer a range of weights and materials. Available nationally, or for a local source, inquire: Peter Storm, Ltd., 126 Davis Ave., Bridgeport, Conn. 06605 (203) 366-5638.

GLOVES, HATS, BAGS, AND BELTS

GLOVES

A fine leather glove is hard to find these days. Just after World War II, there were 200 to 300 glove manufacturers in America, most of them located around Gloversville in upper New York State. Now there are but a handful left. Gloves are no longer *de rigueur* for the well-dressed person and fewer people wear them today than they did in the 1940s. Also, population growth has slowed. Glove sales are centered around a brief six-week period out of the entire year.

In spite of its unassuming appearance, a properly designed glove is actually a very sophisticated piece of clothing engineering. It is subjected to a great deal of stress and strain. It must fit snugly over the hand when relaxed yet stretch to accommodate an increase of an inch in girth and nearly an inch in the length of the back of the hand as the hand is flexed closed.

Glove manufacture (we are talking about quality gloves here) is highly labor intensive and there is no way to automate it. Each glove is cut individually with a die cutter; the leather is first dampened, stretched on the table to work some "give" into the final glove, then die cut. Any scars, thin spots, and other flaws in the leather must be avoided, yet wastage must also be kept to a minimum. The front, back, fingers (which are all cut in a single piece called the "trank"), and the thumb of each glove must all match in color, as must both gloves of each pair. All pieces must also have an equal amount of stretch to them or the gloves will fit poorly. The "fourchettes," which are cut at the same time, are the inserts along the side of each finger which make the glove fit well on the hand. To meet all of these requirements when working with leather, which is not a uniform and perfect man-made material, requires a high degree of skill and knowledge.

Once all the pieces are cut, they are specially stacked together to indicate that these pieces should be used to make a single pair of gloves. Mr. Joe Aulisi, marketing director of Gates-Mills Gloves, told us a story that illustrates the importance of keeping these pieces properly matched. When a whole load of matched pieces was being sent over by truck to the sewing room at his factory, the driver forgot to put up the tailgate and several cartons of glove pieces fell off the truck, spilling their contents over the road. So much for several thousand dollars' worth of gloves; with all the pieces scattered and no longer matched into pairs, they all had to be discarded.

After the gloves are sewn up and any lining inserted, they are then steam-pressed over a glove form to give them their final shape. This finishing stage is known as "laying-off."

One way to judge the quality of a glove is by the feel of the leather. A sign of a really superior glove, rarely seen today, is "quirks." A quirk is a small insert at the base of each finger that allows for greater movement and flexibility.

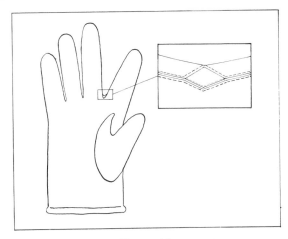

Glove quirk

The shape of the thumb insert tends to vary with quality also. The set-in thumb with a circular seam around the base is generally found on less-expensive gloves; it limits hand movement somewhat and subjects the leather to strain. A French thumb uses a separate quirk between the thumb and index finger to give more room. Best-quality gloves generally use the Bolton or English thumb, which is cut with a triangular projection into the palm and the quirk is cut as part of the main glove. This allows the greatest movement with least strain on the leather.

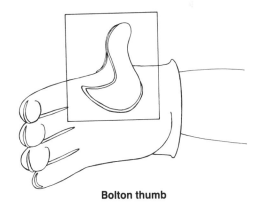

Bolton thumb

Look for reinforcements around buttonholes, snaps, and buttons, and at the wrist opening. A separate binder around the wrist, rather than just a turned up hem, is a stronger construction.

Stitching should be firm, even, and, unless it's intended as decoration, small. Seams may be stitched on either the inside or the outside. Piqué is a very durable seam which is made by lapping one edge of the leather over the other and top-stitching, leaving only one raw edge on the outside. The stitch is very elastic and consequently has long-lasting qualities. On full-piqué gloves, all four seams of each finger are piqué. On half-piqué gloves, only the back seams are piqué and the palm side of the glove is sewn inseam.

Piqué seam

On inseam stitching, the glove is seamed inside out and then turned. This makes a strong, neat stitch that is not visible on the outside.

Outseam includes a variety of different stitches which have in common exposed seam edges. Large, decorative stitches tend to get caught on objects and break.

Leather gloves for milder weather should be bought a trifle snug so they will stretch out and mold to your hand. Gloves for cold weather should never be snug. Deerskin, pigskin, calfskin, and goatskins are all sturdy, long-wearing leathers. The lighter-weight, more pliable skins such as cabretta, capeskin, doe, kid, and mocha are generally used for dressier gloves. All-leather gloves marked "washable," "chrome-tanned," or "oil-tanned" can be washed at home; suede or shearling gloves, lined gloves, and those labeled "dry clean" or "alum-tanned" cannot.

Hand-washing Gloves

Wash gloves in cool water using a very mild soap. We like Nu-Down down cleaner because it is mild and specially formulated to rinse clean.

Although some experts recommend washing gloves on your hands, we have always had good success washing them off our hands. There is the risk that if you wash them on your hands, you will stretch and distort the wet leather as you pull the gloves off.

Wash gloves gently and do not wring or twist. It is important to make certain that all the soap is thoroughly rinsed out. Then gently squeeze out the excess water and lay the gloves flat on a towel. Let them air-dry naturally; *never* place them near any heat.

When they are almost dry, anoint them with a little Lexol leather conditioner to restore any oils lost in washing. Don't try wearing them until they are completely dry. They may feel a little stiff when you first put them on. If necessary, douse them with a little more Lexol. They should quickly soften up again after wearing.

Remember, washing your gloves is never going to restore them to their original pristine appearance. Nothing will do that. And although washing gloves can be beneficial, you don't want to wash them too frequently. Once a year should be ample.

GLOVE SOURCES

Millar leather gloves imported from England have an excellent reputation and come in a wide range of styles. The fingerless mitt shown here has a tough knitted cotton palm and a silicone-treated wool back. Available from REI. $12.   **(Fig. 5-76)**

Angora fingerless mitts, knitted from angora rabbit wool. Silky and smooth to the skin. Available from Marmot Mountain Works. $12.   **(Fig. 5-77)**

Gates-Mills is one of the leading American glove manufacturing companies. They make a range of gloves but the top-quality line is the one we recommend most. From left to right: string glove with goatskin palm and Bolton thumb; knitted wool glove with leather palm; deerskin piqué glove with Bolton thumb. Available nationally, or for a local source, inquire: Gates-Mills Gloves, Johnstown, N.Y. 12095 (518) 762-4526. $25–$40.   **(Fig. 5-78)**

Fig.5-76

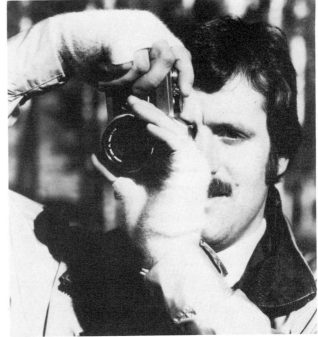

Fig.5-77

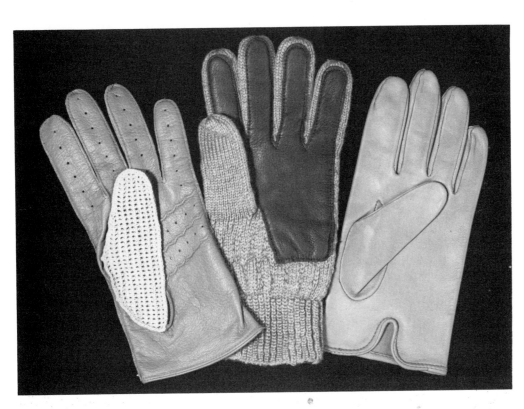

Fig.5-78

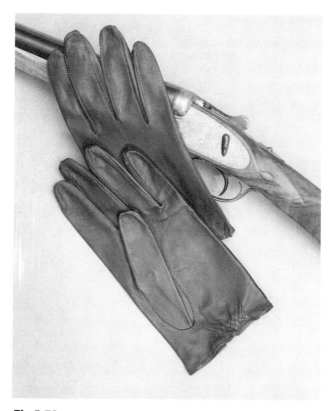

Fig.5-79

Fig.5-80

Capeskin gloves, made of thin capeskin leather, stitched with nylon thread and designed for a snug fit and "bare-hand" feel. Also available in an insulated version with slightly different styling. Available from Orvis. $34. **(Fig.5-79)**

2-in-1 deerskin gloves, for men and women, with adjustable wrist, have separate wool and nylon glove liner inside. Can be worn individually or together. Available from Orvis, Gokeys, and Bauer. $29.   **(Fig. 5-80)**

These wet weather shooting gloves were developed for duck hunters but would be fine for most wet weather uses. The high-quality stretchable deerskin has been specially treated to be waterproof without sacrificing pliability. Available from Orvis. $22.   **(Fig. 5-81)**

Made in England, these gloves for men and women have a smooth cape leather palm for flexibility and sure grip; sheepskin shearling back for warmth. Available from Gokeys. $60.   **(Fig. 5-82)**

Leather mittens, referred to in the trade as choppers, are often used by professional woodsmen and are extremely durable. Made of strong, supple buckskin leather, they have an elasticized wristlet. They also come fully lined with a $^{7}/_{16}$" layer of wool pile. Available from L. L. Bean. $12. Lined, $18.   **(Fig. 5-83)**

Fig.5-81

Fig.5-82

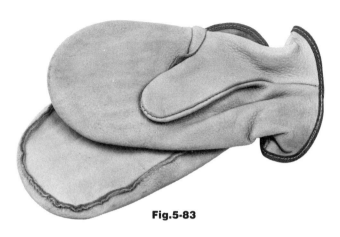

Fig.5-83

HATS

The Hatfield Gore-Tex field hat with leather bill and sweatband. Stuffs easily into bag or jacket pocket. Available from Early Winters. $7.50.   **(Fig. 5-84)**

Fisherman's cap is knit from beige and gray wools in natural colors, no dyes used; 85% wool, 15% nylon for durability. Crush-proof visor. Can be machine-washed in cool water. Storm flap pulls down to keep ears and back of neck warm. Available from Early Winters. $5.   **(Fig. 5-85)**

Fig.5-84

Fig.5-85

Fig.5-86

Fig.5-87

Fig.5-88

Fig.5-89

Brigade Quartermaster carries two excellent berets. The one pictured here is their 100% virgin mothproofed wool basque beret. They also have genuine military berets of 100% virgin wool, fully lined, with leather sweatband. Available from Brigade Quartermaster. $7. **(Fig. 5-86)**

French Creek brings its expertise in shearling and greasewool to hats as well. Here are just four examples.

Men's Ushanka in natural shearling or black Tuscany lamb. Fully lined. Ear flaps tie on top of head or under chin. $50. **(Fig. 5-87)**

Men's Turkoman, piped in leather and fleece-lined. $40. **(Fig. 5-88)**

Astrakhan in soft shearling fleece or black, deep-pile Tuscany lamb (not shown). Fully lined. Can also be ordered to match your French Creek shearling coat. $40. **(Fig. 5-89)**

Alpine is 3-ply greasewool; decorative band can be turned up or worn down. $20. **(Fig. 5-90)**

L. L. Bean claims that this hat, insulated with PolarGuard polyester fiberfill quilted to a rayon lining, will keep your head warm in below 0° F temperatures. Outer shell of 60% combed cotton, 40% nylon. Genuine mouton fur earflaps. Available from L. L. Bean. $14. **(Fig. 5-91)**

A tightly knit 100% wool cap, with a stiffened visor, modeled after the well-known GI helmet liner. This is a very handy cap. Also available in 100% acrylic. Available from L. L. Bean. $6.25. **(Fig. 5-92)**

Fig.5-90

Fig.5-91

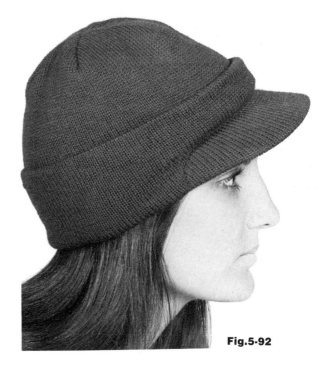

Fig.5-92

Fig.5-93

Fig.5-94

Fig.5-95

Fig.5-96

Fig.5-97

Made in Brittany, France, this cap is 100% tightly woven cotton sailcloth. Available from Norm Thompson. $15.

(Fig. 5-93)

18 oz. 100% cotton duck Plantation hat. 3$^1/_2$" brim has internal wire stiffener that also allows easy shaping. Latigo leather hat band. Available from Eddie Bauer. $16.

(Fig. 5-94)

Mouton storm hat has tuck-away ear flaps of nylon tricot jersey. Available from Eddie Bauer. $30.   **(Fig. 5-95)**

All-shearling trooper hat has flaps and visor that can be worn down to protect ears and forehead. Available from Eddie Bauer. $50.   **(Fig. 5-96)**

Durable fiber mesh hat, molded in traditional pith helmet shape, allows for generous air circulation while still providing ample shade. One size fits all, with adjustable band. Available from Orvis. $9.   **(Fig. 5-97)**

All-cotton safari hat, styled after the famous British Army model. Can be easily rolled up and stuffed in a pocket. Available from Orvis. $16.   **(Fig. 5-98)**

Cattle King by Resistol, one of the finest Western hat makers in America. Fully lined felt hat with 6$^1/_2$" crown, 3$^1/_2$" brim, and 2" headband inside. Available from Norm Thompson. $55.   **(Fig. 5-99)**

Rabbit fur trooper hat. Flaps and visor fold down to protect forehead, neck, and sides of head. Quilt lined, with inner wool earflaps for extra warmth. Available from L. L. Bean. $32.   **(Fig. 5-100)**

Fig.5-98

Fig.5-99

Fig.5-100

Fig.5-101

David Morgan carries some very fine hats including Akubra brand hats from Australia, widely recognized for their quality.

"Aussie" slouch hat by Akubra is the authentic Australian military hat. Pure fur felt, with brass clip and loop to hold the brim up. Puggaree (hat band) and chin strap. $45.   **(Fig. 5-101)**

Sombrero by Akubra is the old-time cowboy hat of pure fur felt. Wide curled brim protects against rain. Calfskin band. $51.   **(Fig. 5-102)**

Bushman by Akubra is the traditional Australian stockman's hat of pure fur felt, fully lined. Shown with David Morgan hand-braided leather hatband. $45.   **(Fig. 5-103)**

Eiger hat of loden cloth with full satin lining. $27.

(Fig. 5-104)

Fig.5-102

Fig.5-103

Fig.5-104

BAGS

Roomy, top grain cowhide carry-all bag. Strong, with reinforced handles. $12 \times 6 \times 12\frac{1}{2}''$ high or $15 \times 7\frac{1}{2} \times 17''$ high. Available from L. L. Bean. Small, $29. Large, $43. **(Fig. 5-105)**

These bags are made from full grain cowhide specially treated to repel stains and water spots. Solid brass hardware, nylon stitching. Firm yet soft leather holds its shape. Scratch marks can be gently rubbed out with your fingertip. Carefully crafted by Michael Green. Available from Norm Thompson. $35–$85. **(Fig. 5-106)**

Made with supple top grain cowhide and careful workmanship, this rucksack is a classic. Padded adjustable shoulder straps, drawcord top; Velcro closure on front and side pockets. Large zippered compartment built into underside of main flap. Available from Norm Thompson. $150. **(Fig. 5-107)**

Fig.5-105

Fig.5-107

Fig.5-106

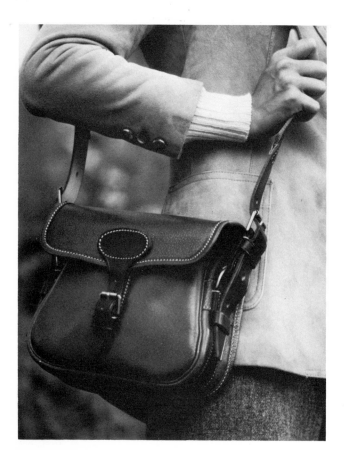

Fig. 5-108

Fig. 5-109

Originally designed as a hunter's shell bag, this bag is made in England of selected pigskin with solid brass fittings. Heavy canvas web shoulder strap. Available from Gokeys. $125.   **(Fig. 5-108)**

Cowhide briefcases, 11½ × 14 × 1½″, with heavy-duty brass zipper. Also in legal size. Available from L. L. Bean. Letter size, $35. Legal, $39.   **(Fig. 5-109)**

BELTS

Australian braided leather cinch ring belt. No stitches to break, no eyelets to tear, continuously adjustable. Available from David Morgan. 1″, $17. 1½″, $22.   **(Fig. 5-110)**

We have some friends who are heavy-duty firearms experts. They tell us point blank that Milt Sparks is one of the world's greatest pistol belt makers. We've seen examples of Mr. Spark's craftsmanship and it's terrific. All custom-made, he will make belts to order without a holster and clip holder. This quality of belt is virtually nonexistent anywhere else—it will last you at least a lifetime. Available from Milt Sparks. $16–$35.   **(Fig. 5-111)**

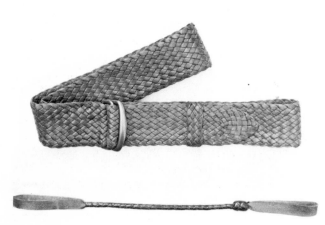

Fig. 5-110

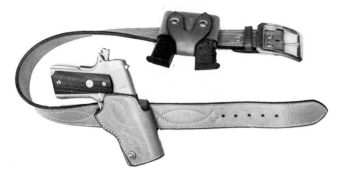

Fig. 5-111

Footwear

THE FOOT

It is estimated that your feet hit the floor an average of 7000 times a day. With each footfall, 26 bones, 60 joints, 112 ligaments, and 20 muscles and tendons move just in the foot, absorbing a total cumulative pressure of some 1000 tons a day. Throughout an average lifetime, your feet will travel 150,000 to 200,000 miles, or six to eight times around the equator.

Footwear must adapt to the foot in movement. For example, if the big toe is squeezed into pointed-toe shoes and pushed out of alignment, it no longer is in the right position to provide proper balance and push-off power.

Although pointed toes, high heels, and platform shoes have been around for many centuries, they never were intended for walking. Historically, they have been a symbol of wealth and superiority, demonstrating that the wearer had no need to be demeaned by walking. Such people instead always had someone to carry them around or a maid or gentleman to support them if they had to take a few steps.

High heels place the foot on an incline from heel to toe, causing the shock of impact and the intended proper distribution of weight to be borne instead by the more delicate forepart of the foot. The bones in the back of the foot are strong, sturdy, and solidly connected; they are designed

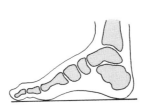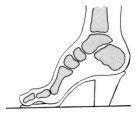

Position of bones in foot normally and when heels are worn

for weight-bearing. The bones in the forefront are far more delicate and made for movement; they are like the fingers of the hand. In bare feet, about 90 percent of the body's weight rests on the heel area; when a high heel is worn, this balance is upset and, the higher the heel, the more that weight rests on the delicate metatarsal bones. Also, the fleshy cushions that normally protect the toes can no longer serve their protective function when the toes are bent in high heels. High heels cause an excessive strain on the lower back and on all the joints up your leg, through your back, and into your neck.

FITTING: GENERAL GUIDELINES

Never, never buy a shoe strictly according to size; always buy on the basis of comfortable fit. An improperly fitted shoe, in addition to being uncomfortable, will wear out much faster than a correctly fitted one. Lasts vary somewhat from one shoe to the next and where you may need a size 8 medium in one shoe, another last will require a size 9. Some lasts will not fit you at all, no matter what size you try on.

Unfortunately, many shoe salespeople do not know how to fit shoes correctly. Because only you can finally determine a shoe's comfort in any case, you have to be the expert.

Try not to buy shoes the first thing in the morning, nor late in the day, especially in hot weather. The average foot increases in volume about 5 percent during a day and twice that in hot weather. Shoes fitted in the morning may later be too snug; those fitted at the end of the day may be too loose for all-day comfort.

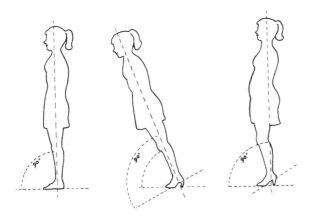

Posture when wearing shoes with high heels

Have both feet measured while you are standing up. It is very likely that both your feet do not measure exactly the same. This is actually quite common, and shoes should be fitted to the larger foot. This measurement, however, is only an approximate *indication* of shoe size. How the shoe feels on your foot is the primary test of whether or not a shoe fits.

In fact, shoes are made on over 10,000 different lasts and in over 300 different sizes in order to fit nearly every foot. Keep in mind that style, materials, and heel height can affect your shoe size from one pair to the next. High heels, for instance, may add as much as a full width to the size you need. Lasts lengthen about $1/3$ inch between whole sizes and increases about $1/4$ inch in girth. This width increase corresponds to about $1/12$ to $1/16$ inch across the flat sole.

Leather will give somewhat but don't buy shoes that feel too tight on the premise that they will eventually stretch out. This is particularly important with synthetic poromeric uppers which, although they give while they are on your feet, will shrink back to their original shape when removed, so the next time you wear the shoes they have to be stretched out all over again. (Poromerics are water-vapor permeable synthetic materials sold under several brand names. Corfam was one of the best known but is no longer on the market.)

A shoe should fit comfortably from the very beginning. You should not have to "break in" your shoes; otherwise, you run the very real risk that your shoes will break your feet before you can break in the shoes. A limited amount of snugness or stiffness is permissible in the beginning. Shoes almost always become more comfortable as your foot gradually molds them to a personalized fit, but it is essential that they also start off being comfortable.

Take time to walk around the store a lot when trying on shoes. Keep in mind that walking on carpet always feels better than walking on hard floors or concrete pavements. Any minor foot discomfort in the shoe store may be multiplied on the street. Also feel inside the shoe for rough stitching or other potential sources of irritation.

When you find a last that fits your foot, we strongly recommend sticking with it. Mark down the shoe manufacturer and design name and, when you buy again, ask for the new shoe designs built over this same last. Shoe salespeople may also know of similar lasts from other manufacturers. Otherwise, contact the manufacturers directly; they should be pleased to help you.

A properly fitted shoe should fit well around the heel of the foot and be kept in position over the arch by laces, straps, or elastic inserts. Providing the fit is good around the heel and the waist, the forepart should be loose, allowing the toes to maintain their proper position and to move freely with walking, and the main part of the foot to swell with heat and exertion.

The shank should give good support and be slightly resilient. If the sole of a shoe can be bent over easily at the in-step or if the waist can be twisted from side to side, however, it will give poor support to the foot. For high-heeled shoes, it's very important that the heel and arch be rigid. If you can flex the heel easily, don't buy the shoe.

Length and breadth must be carefully considered. A shoe that is too short can actually damage your foot, as well as cause discomfort. Shoes must be tried on with the type of socks or stockings you will be wearing with them. While you are standing, check that the length of the shoe and the width across the ball of the foot are correct. There should be a space allowance of between $1/2$ inch and $3/4$ inch between your toes and the end of the shoe. This is because your foot moves forward in the shoe as you walk. Be sure you can wriggle your toes; the toe box should be high enough to exert no pressure on them. If this area is too shallow, a larger size may be worth trying.

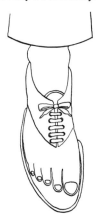

Properly fitted shoe

The width across the ball of the foot should fit with no gapping but also no pressure in order to ensure full function of foot movement in walking. The large and small ball joints of the foot should correspond with the "joint pockets" of the shoe. These are the areas on the inside and outside edge of the sole, where the sole starts to curve under the arch. Neither the big nor the little toes should show through the upper as a bulge. Equally, there should not be a large gap beside either toe because this will cause a deep crease that can cause pain and damage the toes.

The upper should fit smoothly and snugly around the ankle without gapping. To be truly comfortable a shoe should hold the back part of the foot firmly in place while allowing ample room for the toes and ball of the foot. Shoes that are too tight will also make your feet feel cold in the winter.

Shoes with low-cut uppers need to be fitted a little more snugly to prevent the foot from slipping forward in them. In these cases, be sure that the topline or row of decorative stitching does not pass over the big toe joint because the stitching reduces the "give" in the material and the inside may be uncomfortable on some feet. Any slightly tight fit will restrict full foot function and should be avoided wherever possible. Snug heel fit is most important in a high-heeled shoe because this holds the foot in its correct position and prevents it from slipping too far forward into the narrow toe area.

Because the foot is not symmetrical, it is clear that a pointed symmetrical shoe is not a particularly good shape and can cause cramping of the toes and a distortion of the big toe. But a good fit can be obtained with a fairly pointed shoe if it is sufficiently long. If a shoe with a narrow toe area is longer and somewhat deeper than a shoe of the same numerical size with a rounded toe, then the toes need not necessarily be compressed.

This is particularly important for women, whose feet tend to have a somewhat more flexible bony structure, with a big toe somewhat more susceptible to being put out of shape. Another factor is that high heel heights tend to exaggerate the negative effects of a pointed toe because unless the heel effectively grips the foot, there is a tendency for the foot to slip down and the toes to enter the narrow part of the shoe.

After buying a pair of shoes, it is always a good idea to first wear them around the house for a while before wearing them out on the street. This way, if the fit turns out to be uncomfortable, the shoes will still be in good condition to return. Pull an old pair of socks over the shoes as you test them to prevent the soles from getting marred on uncarpeted floors.

Although heel fit should be snug, slight slippage will often occur with a new pair of shoes when the lining is very smooth and the sole is still rigid. This is particularly likely to occur with cowboy boots. If the fit is otherwise correct, and slippage continues, an anti-slip heel liner can be inserted.

A heel topline that cuts into the back of your heel can sometimes be relieved by inserting a heel cushion that lifts the foot a bit and relieves the pressure. If the heel just feels a bit stiff, soften the counter by bending it slightly with the heel of your hand.

If the lacing is too close over the instep on one shoe, so that there is little or no space between the eyelets, but the fit is right otherwise, you can try a tongue pad, which will open up the spacing. Or try using a cushioned insole to raise the foot and instep. This situation generally arises when one foot is quite a bit larger than the other.

SHOE CONSTRUCTION: THE SIX COMMON TYPES

With the **cement construction** shoe, the upper is folded around under a light innersole, then a one-piece outsole is cemented over this. This method, in use since the 1930s, makes possible a light, flexible construction with a small close edge to the sole. There is no stitching, no midsole, and very little support or protection. These shoes are troublesome to resole because once the old sole is removed, there is nothing to hold the shoe's shape while a new sole is being secured. This is a flimsy, inexpensive construction

frequently used on women's fashion shoes and increasingly common on all types of shoes.

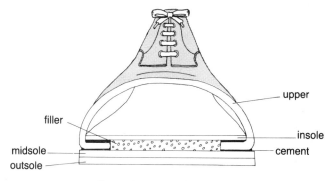

Cement-construction shoe

Injection molding is a relatively recent process, in which the sole and heel are molded and secured to the upper in a single operation, replacing the need for stitching or cement. Sole materials frequently tend to be quite durable and claims are often made that the sole will outlast the upper. However, this is assuming rough wear and minimal care of the upper. If you are interested in keeping your shoes for a long time, you should look for ones with a separate midsole, sandwiched between the upper and the outer sole, so the outer sole can be easily replaced. Although a one-piece molded sole could be ground down by a shoe repairer and a new sole cemented over it, we've never met a good repair person willing to tackle such an ambitious project. Unfortunately, at the present time, injection molding seems to be associated with mass-produced "economy" boots and shoes, and we have been unable to find any top-quality models that use this construction.

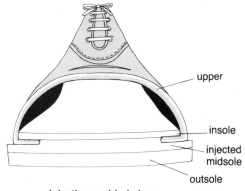

Injection-molded shoe

Inside stitched construction is also known as Littleway, McKay, and American welt, all variations on the same basic method. The upper is turned under and sandwiched between a stout innersole and either a midsole or an outsole. This sandwich is lockstitched together on the inside of the shoe, which protects the stitching from abrasion and dampness. It also allows the sole to be very closely trimmed. Inside stitched construction is more frequently indicative of better and some top-quality shoes.

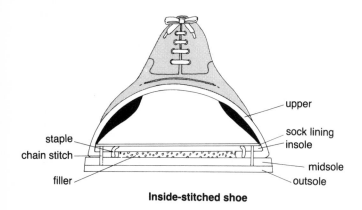

staple
chain stitch
filler
upper
sock lining
insole
midsole
outsole

Inside-stitched shoe

Long recognized as a standard of quality for well-made, water-resistant footwear, the **welt construction** has not changed in basic principle since being perfected over 200 years ago. One of the most common and well-regarded welt constructions is the Goodyear welt, which takes its name from Charles Goodyear, Jr., who developed the first commercial machine that could successfully duplicate the complex hand motions made while sewing the welt to the bottom.

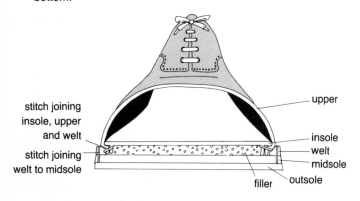

stitch joining
insole, upper
and welt
stitch joining
welt to midsole
upper
insole
welt
midsole
outsole
filler

Goodyear welt-construction shoe

This construction can be made very flexible and is comfortable, durable, and easily repaired. Two lines of stitching are used to attach the sole to the upper. The first hidden inseam secures the upper and the welt (a narrow strip of leather) to the specially ribbed insole. This leaves the top or foot side of the innersole free from stitches or tacks and completely smooth to the foot. Also, no sock liner is required to cover thread or metal. Then the outseam lockstitches the outersole to the protruding welt, thus securing the sole to the upper.

Shoes made by this method can be easily repaired and will retain their shape better than any other construction, even after many resolings. A well-made shoe of this type is very water-repellent and is comfortable because of the cushioning filler in the cavity between sole and innersole. A

tremendous degree of highly skilled work goes into making these shoes, and materials must be of good quality. Goodyear welt construction is becoming increasingly expensive and increasingly rare so we would recommend you invest now while you still have the chance.

Mock welts imitate the look of the welted shoe but these welts serve no function, so beware—ask questions.

In the **stitchdown construction**, often seen on desert boots, the upper is simply turned or flanged out over the top of the sole extension and stitched to the sole. This method may incorporate a midsole and also a mock welt.

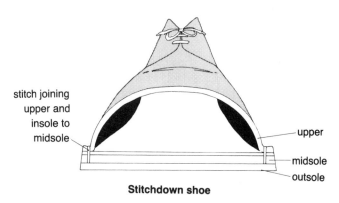

stitch joining
upper and
insole to
midsole
upper
midsole
outsole

Stitchdown shoe

A true **moccasin construction**, which has been in use for several thousand years, consists of a single, unseamed piece of leather that cradles the bottom of the foot and wraps around to form the sides of the shoe. The plug, which covers the top of the foot, is then hand- or machine-sewn to this main piece. This construction provides a "hammock" for the foot, with no separate innersole to curl up or break so the bottom is permanently level and smooth.

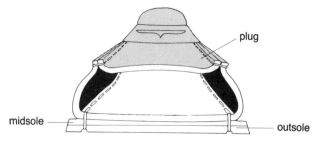

midsole
plug
outsole

True moccasin construction

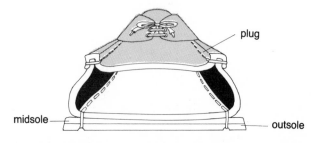

midsole
plug
outsole

More weatherproof version of moccasin construction

Because a moccasin left like this would afford little protection on pavements, either for the foot or the shoe, a separate sole and sometimes midsole is added.

Moccasin-type stitching on the front of a shoe is often used on other constructions just for styling, and by itself is no indication of a true moccasin.

CARE FOR LONG SHOE LIFE

As we've indicated before, the general quality of shoes has been declining steadily. The footwear in this book represents an exception to that fact, so one of the first best steps to take for long shoe life is to invest in high-quality shoes and boots.

Secondly, and this is important, it makes a lot of sense to own a number of pairs of shoes. The more shoes you have, the easier it is to distribute wear over all of them. It makes little sense to own only one or two pairs of extremely good shoes which you wear constantly and, although they may serve you valiantly, will nevertheless go to an early grave. In fact, it is a very bad practice to wear the same pair of shoes two days in a row. Remember, the foot produces a lot of perspiration and after a long, hard day, a shoe or boot should be given 24 hours to dry out. So an important part of caring for your shoes is ensuring that each pair does not receive excessive use.

Another fundamental credo of shoe care is to wear the appropriate shoe at the appropriate time. Don't wear your Allen Edmonds Austins in the rain, unless you consciously don't give a damn about ruining them. We regularly see people slopping around in the snow and slush wearing very expensive cowboy boots, and we groan in sorrow. Even such rugged models as the Lotus Veldtschoen or a Russell birdshooter, although designed for heavy-duty treatment, deserve to be spared unnecessary punishment. Better to set aside your Russells on a wet day and wear your Bean rubber-bottom hunting boots.

The less abuse a shoe receives, the longer its life. It's that simple. The object is not to Baha-roadtest your footwear but to allow it, through conscientious management, to live out its fullest possible lifespan. At least that's the way we see it.

Therefore, strange as it may at first seem, the trick to getting the most from high-quality durable shoes is to treat them as gently as possible. Keep them clean, lubricated, and in good repair. When you take off your shoes, give them a quick dusting with a soft cloth or clean shoe brush—dirt acts as an abrasive. It works its way into the leather and erodes the fibrous structure of the leather. Also, perspiration from your feet does, over time, have a deleterious effect on leather. So don't wear your street shoes when you don't need to indoors; change into a pair of house shoes or slippers.

Clean your shoes and boots thoroughly on a regular basis. Even if you wear your shoes only for street wear, you should still clean them often. Shoes worn for more rugged purposes should be cleaned much more frequently. Not only does dust and dirt work its way into the leather, but water and airborne pollutants also have a destructive effect on leather.

On nonsuede shoes and boots of quality leather, use paste saddlesoap and water. We don't recommend liquid or foam saddlesoap. One of the best saddlesoaps we know of is Fiebing's. Work it up into a rich lather over the leather, wipe it off, then rinse thoroughly, using a damp cloth. Turn the cloth frequently so as to always use a clean part of it. Work fairly quickly because both the soap and the water are drying to leather. Be sure to clean carefully where the upper and sole join and in other similar areas where dirt tends to accumulate.

The leather must then be reconditioned to restore the necessary oils. We've always been very satisfied with Lexol, which is frequently recommended by leather care experts. Lexol is also excellent for cleaning and reconditioning the leather lining inside your shoes.

Then, if you want a shine, wax your shoes. Paste wax, such as Kiwi or Kelly's Lynn, not only imparts a gloss but also provides some surface protection against dirt and moisture. For a semigloss shine, or on porous leathers such as oil-tanned leather, apply a shoe cream.

Suede shoes must be treated somewhat differently. Condition the leather from the *inside* with a product such as Lexol. To keep them looking neat, brush up the nap with a nylon or rubber bristle brush. If bald patches appear, try rubbing very gently with fine emery paper until the nap is raised. In general, suede shoes are hard to keep looking spiffy.

If your shoes or boots do get wet, immediately wipe off the water and any mud as soon as you get back indoors, to prevent further absorption into the leather. The next step is to let the boots dry thoroughly before wearing them again. If it takes three days for them to dry completely, then wait three days.

Never, never, ever quick-dry your shoes or boots by placing them on or even near a radiator or other heat source. Heat, especially for wet shoes, spells death to leather. Air-dry them at room temperature only. Be sure to put shoe trees in them or stuff them with paper to help maintain their shape.

When the shoes begin to become fairly dry, apply some Lexol. Once the shoes are completely dry, inspect the leather and, if it looks or feels stiff, apply some neat's-foot oil, mink oil, or other conditioner.

The market is absolutely crammed with a variety of shoe-care products. It is very important to select and use only those products that are of a reputable quality. Cheap, poorly formulated dressings and cleaners will do nothing but cause injury.

It is also important not to overdo it with shoe-care products because excessive treatments can oversoften the leather and cause heel counters and toe boxes to break down, and once this happens, your shoes have had it.

When applying dressings such as mink oil or dubbin, we find that it helps significantly to warm up the dressing until it melts and then baste it on with a cloth or brush. This greatly facilitates absorption of the dressing well into the leather. This holds especially true for products such as Sno-Seal, a very good quality snow- and water-repellent.

Water and the various pollutants and chemicals that are often dissolved in water damage leather. Water itself softens leather, causing the fibers to stretch and break under strain. It also drives out the essential emollients impregnated during the tanning process, causing the leather to dry out and become embrittled. In our experience, there is no such thing as a totally waterproof leather. There are just leathers that are more water resistant than others. In our opinion, *no* leather, even high-quality water-resistant leather, should be exposed unnecessarily to water saturation. In addition, no waterproofing preparation that we know of can guarantee leather complete protection from water damage.

From our experience, Sno-Seal, a siliconized wax, is one of the finest heavy-duty water proofers available. Because it is a wax, it does not lubricate leather and a conditioner must be applied periodically. Most conditioners will penetrate through Sno-Seal but it is generally advisable to recoat lightly with Sno-Seal after conditioning. (A light recoating can be done directly from the can, without having to melt the wax.) Beware: Sno-Seal has a distinct tendency to darken some leathers, especially lighter-colored ones. Sno-Seal is a heavy-duty, water-repelling product and we don't feel it is suited for such things as dress shoes or fancy Western boots, and so on. Shoes treated with Sno-Seal also tend to be hotter in the summer.

Liquid silicone is another water repellent. In our opinion, it is not as effective as Sno-Seal and does not last as long. It is a lot less messy to apply, however, does not darken leather as much, and is definitely appropriate for dress shoes and other fancy footwear. Like Sno-Seal, it makes shoes hotter in the summer.

Some of the following quality leather-care products act as conditioners as well as medium-duty water repellents.

Mink Oil is a popular and very well-respected conditioner. We personally have a preference for Original Mink Oil brand because, as far as we know, it contains the highest percentage of actual mink renderings. Best applied melted. Offers good protection against water exposure but is not, in our judgment, sufficient protection against prolonged soakings.

Leath-r-seal is a most excellent water repellent and leather preservative.

Neat's-foot oil is an excellent leather preservative with light-duty water repellent characteristics. We recommend using only *pure* neat's-foot oil; neat's-foot oil *compounds* are best avoided. In the old days, neat's-foot oil had the disadvantage of deteriorating cotton or linen thread but new refining techniques have eliminated this problem.

Another good conditioner and water repellent is *dubbin*. Theoretically, dubbin can be made from any number of substances but the one we prefer is made from the greases extracted from sheep's wool. One of the best dubbins we've encountered is available by mail from M. J. Knoud Saddlery, 716 Madison Avenue, New York, N.Y. 10021 (212) 838-1434.

Peter Limmer, one of this country's premier boot makers (see p. 134), sells his own special homemade secret concoction called *Peter Limmer's Boot Grease*. Given Mr. Limmer's enormous expertise and dedication to integrity and quality, we decided to try it out. Results were very positive. It also imparts a pleasing sheen.

SHOE REPAIR

It shouldn't surprise you to read that any shoes worth their salt must be kept in good repair if you expect them to last. With shoes, as with so many other things in life, anticipating and promptly treating a problem before it develops any further is the smartest approach.

So, keeping your shoes properly maintained at some point must invariably involve the services of a top-quality shoe repairer. We say top quality because placing any shoes in the hands of a less than fully competent repairer is courting disaster and that's not an exaggeration—we've painfully learned this by having shoes effectively ruined by well-intentioned but nevertheless clumsy tradesmen.

Back in the "old days," skilled shoe repairers and even shoemakers were quite common and, as a result, their services came relatively cheap. Today, regrettably, this is definitely not the case. Highly qualified shoe repairers are artisans who cannot possibly have learned their craft without years of thoughtful effort. Such skilled people deserve not only your respect for their achievement but also fair and adequate monetary compensation.

Finding one of these repairers is a very ticklish matter but an unavoidable one. Repair people who make custom shoes would certainly be a good bet. Otherwise, you must unfortunately proceed on your instincts. Naturally, a recommendation from a friend or acquaintance may steer you straight. Certainly the proprietor of any high-quality shoe store should be able to offer a good referral. But do be cautious—check the repairer's work; don't bring in your favorite shoes for a major resoling job on your first visit.

There is one preventive maintenance procedure that we advocate most strongly. It is inexpensive to perform and makes an enormous contribution toward the longest possible life of shoes and boots. This is the tap sole or, as we like to call it, the martyr sole. Very simply it consists of having a repairperson glue a thin rubber half-sole over the existing outer sole. This procedure is best performed on new shoes before they are ever worn. It's somewhat harder to get the glue to adhere to a sole that's known pavement.

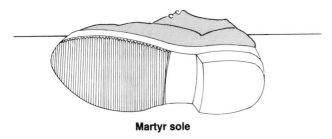

Martyr sole

The advantage of adding this sole is that it, instead of the main sole, suffers the punishment of daily wear. Resoling a shoe or boot is an expensive and sometimes somewhat risky proposition. By adding a martyr sole, the main sole never has to be replaced. When the martyr sole wears down, it is easily peeled off and a new one glued on.

Shoes with leather heels should have a rubber lift added; again, so the lift can be sacrificed instead.

Here are the names of four highly regarded shoe repairers. The first three we can vouch for from personal experience.

Elio Floro of Syosset has won numerous awards for his skills and is expert at orthopedic work as well. He also makes absolutely fantastic custom-made shoes—they are, of course, very expensive. He gladly accepts mail-order repair jobs. Steve Komito is nationally known for hiking and mountain boot repairs and was recommended to us by a number of highly respected sources. He accepts mail-order assignments. White's not only repairs shoes but makes them as well; some of their shoes are shown in this book.

Syosset Shoe Shop
Elio Floro
37 Berry Hill Road
Syosset, N.Y. 11791
(516) 921-4747

James Custom Shoe Repair Shop
Nick Pecchia
102 East 87 St
New York, N.Y. 10028
(212) 722-0041
No mail order.

Frank's Custom Shoe Repair
Frank Petro
1070 Madison Ave
New York, N.Y. 10028
(212) 288-1439
No mail order.

Komito Boots
Steve Komito
P.O. Box 2106
Estes Park, Colo. 80517
(303) 586-5391

White's Shoe Shop
430 West Main
Spokane, Wash. 99201
(509) 624-3731

Top-Sider also maintains a listing of shoe repairers all over the country who will resole and repair Top-Sider footwear. For the name of the repairer near you, contact:

Sperry Top-Sider, Inc.
P.O. Box 2107
Richmond, Indiana 47374
(317) 935-7391

When buying shoes, here are the quality points to check for:

Trendy styling commonly means that quality has been sacrificed for fashion. Manufacturers expect such shoes to go out of style quickly and construct them accordingly.

In general, you want an all-leather construction, including innersole, midsole heel counter, toe box, and lining. Synthetic materials in our experience just don't stand up as well and are not as comfortable.

Elio Floro, nationally recognized as one of the country's foremost shoe repairers, stresses that the foundation of a good shoe is a sturdy sole construction with a firm shank, strong heel counter, and toe box.

Goodyear welt construction is highly desirable. On any construction, always look for a midsole because this allows shoes to be repaired far more easily.

Vibram soles, made in the United States by the Quabaug Rubber Company of North Brookfield, Massachusetts, are of notably high quality—one of the top names in shoe soles. However, the presence of Vibram soles in no way automatically indicates that a boot or shoe is of equally high quality.

The fewer the seams in a pair of shoes, especially seams that are simply decorative, the fewer areas where seams can fail. For example, Clark's makes two kinds of Treks: one kind has a single-piece vamp construction; the other uses a two-piece vamp construction seamed down the center of the vamp. In our experience, this center seam eventually fails; the single-piece vamp construction considerably outlasts the two-piece vamp.

Decorations and doodads on the whole are just so much gingerbread—they cost extra and make no practical contribution. Just as importantly, they're an additional area where things can go wrong.

Check that all hardware, including grommets, buckles, D-rings, and so on is firmly secured and strong enough to last. We've seen shoes which upon closer inspection revealed that the buckles were stapled on instead of being stitched.

BUYING BY MAIL

Even in a city the size of New York, certain premier brands of footwear are not locally available. So yes, buying shoes by mail is a perfectly sensible and in many cases a highly desirable practice.

Shoe companies such as W. C. Russell, Peter Limmer, and Randal Merrell, to name just a few, as well as many mail-order houses, guarantee a correct fit or your money back. Not only that but if the shoes ever prove faulty (excluding mistreatment), your money is refunded. That's a much better offer than many local merchants are prepared to make.

As far as fit goes, it may require time and a little patience but we have each purchased several pairs by mail-order with very satisfactory results. If possible, it may be advisable to order two pairs of the same shoe a half-size apart, so you have a better opportunity to compare fit. Then just return the extra pair.

Sending a tracing of your foot is always preferable. Randal Merrell has contributed this special tip. Get hold of some goldenrod mimeograph paper, available at stationary stores. This paper changes color to bright red when moistened with a solution of water and baking soda. Just sponge the bottom of your foot with a baking soda solution, step on the paper and then, without moving your foot, take a tracing, being very careful to hold the pencil vertical to the paper. Don't worry, the red will not come off on your foot. This method provides much more accurate information than just a tracing alone. However, please note: Some types of goldenrod mimeo do not react to baking soda. Seek and ye shall find—it's pretty common.

FOOTWEAR SOURCES

Randal Merrell is one of America's finest custom boot builders. His devotion to quality and excellence are truly inspiring. Like Peter Limmer, he could, if he wanted to, go mass production but his personal integrity and pride demand that he do the finest job he knows how. So Mr. Merrell builds each boot from scratch, custom work only.

Mr. Merrell is not just a boot builder; he is an artisan who produces truly superlative work. He fully guarantees a comfortable fit and his experience has been that custom fitting by mail on his hiking boots presents few problems. Out of 100, only three or four pairs may need to be remade.

Randal also makes absolutely superb custom Western boots. But fitting them is much trickier and he will only make you a pair if he has personally taken the measure of your feet. Merrell's reputation is such that people gladly pay his airfare for him to come to their homes to measure them.

He'll fit any foot you can offer: size 18, AAAA or EEEEEEEEE (which he has made), one shoe in a size 8 and the other in size 10, if that's what the customer needs.

Mr. Merrell has put together a very detailed and extremely instructive information packet which contains explicit instructions for measuring your feet.

In our eyes, there could never be an excess of people like Randal Merrell in this world.

Three examples of boots are shown, available from Randal Merrell.

This hiking boot is Mr. Merrell's completely original design. Among its special features are a one-piece upper, with only a single seam; a unique one-piece lining, with the seam placed so the foot never touches it; a heavy leather counter to eliminate the common problem of the lining quickly wearing out at the heel. Both heel counter and insole are made of thick oak-tanned leather for long-lasting wear.

Fig.6-1

Fig.6-2

The back of the boot is curved to conform to your foot to prevent rubbing, slipping, and blistering. The steel shank is round instead of flat to improve support and is individually shaped to each boot.

Mr. Merrell uses only the best parts of top grain Latigo cowhide; he personally selects each hide from a small tannery in Utah. Every stitch is a lockstitch and only nylon and polyester thread are used. Each pair of Merrell boots takes several weeks to build. $320.* **(Figs. 6-1,2,3)**

*Prices listed are approximate and as of September 1980.

Mr. Merrell also came up with this unique design. With these Velcro closures instead of laces, the boots can be put on and removed in a few seconds. Also, any part of the boot can be made tighter or looser independently of the other parts. A special anti-peel tab precludes the risk of the straps peeling loose. This feature is offered for an added charge of $35 on any boot. **(Fig. 6-4)**

Here is an example of one of Merrell's exquisite custom Western boots. $380 and up. **(Fig. 6-5)**

Fig.6-3

Fig.6-4

Fig.6-5

Fig.6-6

Steve Komito of Komito Boots has specialized in the sale and repair of mountain footwear for more than a decade. He and his staff are dedicated to a standard of excellence and have a nationwide, if not international, reputation, especially for boot repair. When you send him your boots to be repaired, specify exactly what you would like done, so as to give Mr. Komito an idea of what kind and how extensive a repair job you want. In order to maintain smooth operations and minimize the amount of time boots remain in his shop, he asks that you first write a letter to schedule an appointment.

In addition to quality work and expertise, Mr. Komito also offers courtesy and consideration at no additional cost. Everyone we know who's dealt with Mr. Komito says that he's a very considerate man, especially of his customers. Incidentally, his store is open seven days a week.

He sells in his shop and by mail-order an excellent line of outdoor boots, boot care, and foot care products, and replacement soles, specifically Galibiers and an assortment of Vibrams. Shown are three of the boots he carries.

Boot repair area at Komito Boot Shop.   **(Fig. 6-6)**

Fig.6-7

Kastinger Kletterschue: for trail hiking and moderate rock climbing. McKay welt with leather midsole; split leather upper. $60. **(Fig. 6-7)**

Desert Fox: lightweight boot for trail and moderate rock climbing. Split leather upper; leather and canvas lined. Lightly padded around the ankle, with lightly padded tongue. Welted construction; rubber midsole; Vibram Roccia sole. $50. **(Fig. 6-8)**

Kastinger Horizon: very lightweight for general hiking and mountaineering purposes. Welted construction with rubber midsole and Vibram Roccia sole. Full grain leather upper, rough side out. Lightly padded ankle and tongue. Tongue is sewn to upper with gussets along half its length. Leather can be waxed for good water resistance. $90. **(Fig. 6-9)**

Fig.6-8

Fig.6-9

Fig.6-10

Fig.6-11

Fig.6-12

Peter Limmer and Sons Inc. is unquestionably one of America's premier boot crafters. It's probably safe to say that Peter Limmer, along with Randal Merrell of Utah (see p. 130) are the two finest handmade hiking boot builders in the entire country and probably North America. If you're looking for superior excellence at an exceptionally reasonable price, Peter Limmer is your man. Given conscientious care, a pair of his boots, especially if worn only for street use, will last 25 years.

Mr. Limmer confines his best efforts (which are his only efforts) to two boot models, one custom-fitted, the other imported exclusively by him from Bavaria. Mr. Limmer's experience with custom fitting by mail has been a 97 percent successful fit. He says there are no problems if a person is meticulous in measuring. If he doesn't get the fit right on the first pair, Mr. Limmer will make another. If the second pair doesn't fit, he'll make a third, all at no extra charge to the customer. After that, he throws in the towel.

The sole has a rocker design built into it which makes the boot easier to break in and more comfortable to wear. The sole is firmly secured to the innersole with cadmium plated screws. In addition, he uses only one major seam on the upper, which is a more expensive method but creates fewer seams to open or rot out.

After five generations of his family in the shoemaking profession, Peter Limmer should know what he's doing—and clearly he does. He thrives on the satisfaction of making a good product. Limmer boots are available directly from Peter Limmer and Sons in Intervale, New Hampshire, and come in up to size 16 and in AAAA to EEEE widths.

A Peter Limmer boot. Custom-made, $125. Stock shoe, $90.   **(Fig. 6-10)**

The Stewart Boot Company is another name that comes very highly recommended. It's a small operation where each pair is made completely by one person and involves about 300 individual steps.

Mr. Victor Borg, the president, takes enormous pride in the accomplishments of his company and the team of craftsmen who produce truly excellent footwear.

Stewart is the only quality outfit we know of that specializes in horsehide. Good horsehide is hard to find these days and just as hard to wear out.

Premium quality all-leather materials and full glove leather lining are standard on all Stewarts. Workmanship is laudable and sizes range from 3½ to 14, A–EEE, men's and women's.

Available nationally, or for a local source, inquire: Stewart Boot Company, 30 West 28 Street, Tucson, Ariz. 85713, (602) 791-9973

Sperry Top-Sider has been one of the most famous names in boating footwear since 1934. Sperry offers a lifetime guarantee. Also, you can mail in Top-Siders to specially authorized repair people who will fully refurbish and resole them. Write to Sperry Top-Sider, P.O. Box 338, Naugatuck, Conn. 06770 (203) 729-0261 to find the names of the repairers in your area.

Sperry leathers are specially tanned to withstand repeated wettings and exposure to brine, making them an excellent choice for wet weather shoes. Their patented sole offers additional protection on slippery surfaces.

The main point though is that Top-Siders are still made with real quality and, if you should ever find otherwise, inform Top-Sider pronto.

Available from L. L. Bean, Eddie Bauer, Lands' End, and Gokeys.

Four examples are shown.

Classic leather moccasins for men and women. $50. **(Fig. 6-11)**

Sea Mate—heavy sailcloth upper, double cushioned arch. $25. **(Fig. 6-12)**

Canvas Oxford—the original Top-Sider. $25. **(Fig. 6-13)**

Top-Sider over-the-sock boot, available in 9″ (women), 11″, and 14″ heights. Also foam-insulated Snug Harbor model in 11″ height. Women's, $40. Men's, $42. Snug Harbor, $52. **(Fig. 6-14)**

This reasonably priced sports sandal has rubber soles, a leather insole covered with a layer of foam and suede leather for comfort. Insole and oil-tanned leather straps are permanently bonded to sole. Brass plated buckles and rivets. Available from Eddie Bauer. $20. **(Fig. 6-15)**

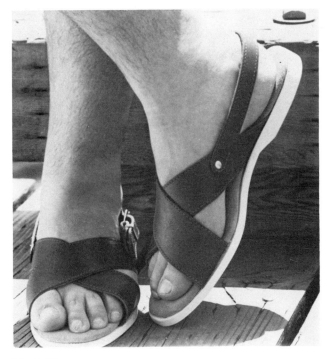

Fig. 6-15

Fig. 6-13

Fig. 6-14

Fig.6-16

Fig.6-17

One of the most highly respected men's dress shoe companies, E. T. Wright, manufactures Wright Arch Preserver Shoes. Their name was consistently recommended to us by even their competitors. Wright uses a special construction innersole designed to support the metatarsal region of the foot. Construction is all Goodyear welt and quality of workmanship and materials is all high caliber.

Styling tends to be somewhat bourgeois at times but we've included two examples of their more classic models. An excellent shoe that's worth every cent you pay for it. Available nationally.

Style 149 Also available with full double sole. $94.

(Fig. 6-16)

Style 128 Oil-tanned leather upper; composition sole. $87.　　　　　　　　　　　　　　　　**(Fig. 6-17)**

Mr. Leon L. Bean developed his now-famous Maine Hunting Shoe back in 1912, when he saw the need for a lightweight, waterproof, and rugged boot. He came up with an exceptionally practical and now frequently copied innovation. That's not to say that there aren't a few good copies here and there. Something we particularly like about the Bean shoe is that it's built on a rocker last, which means the sole is curved upward to provide spring to your step, thus avoiding the flat-footed, clumping effect found in chintzier, less well thought out versions.

Bean has since branched out into moccasins, Vibram-soled hunting shoes, and even a felt-lined pac model, among others. Four examples are shown, available from L. L. Bean.

Lounger Boot. 7″, $36. 9″, $41.　　　　　**(Fig. 6-18)**

Vibram Soled Maine Hunting Shoe. $56.　　**(Fig. 6-19)**

The GumShoe. $34.　　　　　　　　　　　**(Fig. 6-20)**

Classic Maine Hunting Shoe. 6″, $35. 16″, $60.　**(Fig. 6-21)**

Fig.6-18

Gokeys has built their reputation principally around their unusual line of handmade boots and shoes. We've never had any experience with them personally but we've heard a number of very encouraging testimonials. Gokeys has assured us that they have a 100 percent satisfaction guaranteed policy. Made with a true moccasin construction and waterproof welt, these boots and shoes, although they may seem expensive, should serve you well for many years and prove in the long run to be a distinctly frugal investment. Widths up to EE on some styles. Available from Gokeys.

Gokeys Sauvage Oxfords for men and women. True moccasin construction. 6 oz. leather uppers with crepe soles. Men's, $70. Women's, $65. **(Fig. 6-22)**

Fig.6-19

Fig.6-20

Fig.6-21

Fig.6-22

Fig. 6-23

Fig. 6-24

Redwing is known throughout many parts of the country as a dependable, serviceable, quality boot and work shoe manufacturer. They have a price and quality range that varies but their top of the line Goodyear welt models are certainly quite respectable. We've always found the Redwing stores to be well-staffed and serviced. If you've just gotten into town, the manager of the local Redwing store probably knows the name of the best shoe repair person in the area.

A division of Redwing is the Vasque Boot Company. They manufacture a variety of hiking and specialty boots for outdoor sports. But some of their lighter-duty models would make excellent choices for daily wear. Definitely dependable quality. Available nationally and selected models available from Holubar, REI, and EMS.

Vasque Chukka-lug, also available in low-cut version. 6″ full grain water-resistant leather upper with leather storm welt. Leather lined quarters. Vibram honey-colored lug sole. $66.   **(Fig. 6-23)**

Redwing #947 8″ workboot with full grain oil-tanned upper. Reinforced heel counter and ankle. Inside arch lift. Composition nitrile and rubber cork sole. $60.   **(Fig. 6-24)**

The Joseph M. Herman Shoe Company has been making rugged footwear since 1879. For many years a principle supplier to the military, Herman's is today best known for their Survivor line, which is one of the best mass-produced boot lines around. Four examples are shown. Available nationally.

Style 7193 Full grain cowhide upper; full grain glove leather lining. Ensolite foam insulation protects to -20° F. Genuine Goodyear leather welt; extra heavy midsole; Vibram sole. $100.   **(Fig. 6-25)**

Style 7174 Full grain oil-tanned upper; Ensolite foam insulation; heavy-duty brass rings and hooks, $110. **(Fig.6-26)**

Style 7156 Silicone treated leather uppers; brass eyelets; Ensolite insulation good to -20° F; Vibram sole. $80.   **(Fig. 6-27)**

Style 7127 Lightweight field shoes. $76.   **(Fig. 6-28)**

Fig.6-25

Fig.6-26

Fig.6-27

Fig.6-28

Fig.6-29

Fig.6-30

Fig.6-32

Fig.6-31

One of the "last of the Mohicans," the W. C. Russell Moccasin Co. is a legend in its own time. Makers of primo quality moccasins, boots, and oxfords for men and women. When ordered directly from the Russell company, each order is individually made up to your personal foot specifications.

Russell uses only the choicest leathers. Craftsmanship and finish work are a pleasure to behold. With tender loving care, who knows how long a pair of theirs will last you. Russell is one of the few companies that offers double vamp construction, that is, the body of the shoe is essentially two shoes in one. On their boots, the uppers and lowers are hand-sewed together with double lockstitching.

No matter what kind of foot you have, as long as it's recognizable as a foot, Russell should be able to accommodate you nicely. If you really appreciate true craftsmanship and functional integrity, we strongly recommend you contact Russell soon because leather prices continue to climb.

Their catalog and order form are pretty explicit, although the catalog could definitely be a little more detailed. Nevertheless, with it in hand, you can get a far better feel for what this truly remarkable company can offer you.

P.S. If you've got Russells, treat them with respect.

Available from W. C. Russell Moccasin Co. Selected models also available from Eddie Bauer, Orvis, and Staffords.

Four examples are shown.

Snake boot of 10 oz. bullhide leather. Double vamp construction with sealed seams, oak-tanned leather counters. Hand-stitched vamps and toe piece. $165.   **(Fig. 6-29)**

Cavalier: Available with double or single vamp construction. Uppers made of choicest grade veal leather. Oak-tanned leather counters. Single vamp, $86. Double vamp, $97.   **(Fig. 6-30)**

Imperial: A boot to set standards by. Upper of choice water-resistant veal leather. Double vamp construction. Oak-tanned leather counters. $99.   **(Fig. 6-31)**

Oneida for men, women, and children. Genuine moccasin construction. Double layer sole can be replaced by Russell as needed. Lightweight flexible comfort. Can be special ordered with low heels. $48.   **(Fig. 6-32)**

Made in France, the Palladium is a comfortable, lightweight boot with thick molded rubber lug sole and upper of heavy duck backed with cotton drill. Double-stitched seaming, part-bellows tongue, removable hemp innersole.

African Safari people swear by this boot. Clarks once did a version of it called the Rhino which was also very highly thought of. The nice thing about the Rhino was that it was available in both high top and low cut. Unfortunately, Clarks seems to have discontinued production, at least in the United States.

We had a lot of trouble getting further information about the Palladium from the American importers, Jacques Cohen in New York City.

Palladiums are a blessed alternative to those multicolored flimsy things that try to pass as sneakers. Available from Orvis and L. L. Bean.

The Palladium lightweight boot for men and women. $30.   **(Fig. 6-33)**

Fig.6-33

Fig.6-34

Fig.6-37

Fig.6-35

Fig.6-38

Fig.6-36

Here's another one of those rare bird companies. Run by Mr. Bill Danner and his son Pete, it produces some of America's finest hiking, logging, and trail footwear for men and women. Real, uncompromising quality for an honest dollar. Although as far as we know, they don't do any custom work, they'll fit you or be hanged trying. A broad selection of sizes and widths. Top quality materials and artisan's workmanship.

Available nationally or from Danner; selected models from Eddie Bauer, REI, L. L. Bean, Norm Thompson, and Todd's.

Shown are five examples of Danner boots.

Forest Trail for men and women: We've got a pair of these and they are very comfortable. Vibram Silvato crepe sole provides good cushioning and wears well. Available from Eddie Bauer and Norm Thompson. Also available directly from Danner with Vibram lug sole. $67. **(Fig. 6-34)**

Ranch boots combine the best features of a Western boot and a lace-up work boot. Double leather vamps; heavy leather insole and midsole with Vibram non-lug sole. $90. **(Fig. 6-35)**

Mountain Trail boots for men and women. Widely considered one of the finest mass-production boots of its kind available in the United States. Durable full grain upper, leather-lined, padded ankle and tongue. Nickel D-rings and hooks. "Yellow Label" Vibram Montagna lug soles and heels. $80. **(Fig. 6-36)**

Two new offerings from Danner are a lightweight version of their trail boot, the Urban Walker ($74), and a canvas and leather warm weather boot, The Fossil ($83). **(Figs. 6-37, 38)**

Marine Corps friends of ours swear by Corcoran jump boots. They tell us that once a paratrooper gets out of jump school, one of his first moves is to scrap Uncle Sam's GI issue boots and invest in a pair of Corcorans.

Jack Bernstein, owner of Gyro Surplus Corporation in New York City, and a well-known military surplus authority, declares that Corcorans are the best American-made boots available.

They are built entirely of top quality leather and expertly constructed. These boots were originally designed for the kind of people who don't fool around, especially with junky imitations. Available nationally or from U.S. Cavalry Store. $65. **(Fig. 6-39)**

The Fallschirmspringerstiefel German paratrooper boot is considered by many the ultimate jump boot. Calfskin-lined, protective padding around ankle. Special water-repellent leather; leather innersole and welt; leather outsole. Double-stitched throughout. Available from Brigade Quartermaster. $125. **(Fig. 6-40)**

Fig. 6-39

Fig. 6-40

Fig.6-41

Fig.6-42

Fig.6-43

Fig.6-44

Fig.6-45

Fig.6-46

In Texas, success means owning a pair of Luccheses, not a Cadillac. Lucchese prides itself on having been the bootmaker for John Wayne and Lyndon Johnson, among other famous names.

For decades, the name Lucchese has meant the absolute finest in Western boots. Although Lucchese was bought out recently by the Blue Bell (Wrangler) company, the general feeling among our consultants is that Lucchese still ranks at the top of the list despite some concern that Blue Bell may be initiating some changes.

Predominantly hand-crafted, Luccheses are made with the finest leathers. The leather soles are hand-rubbed with color, rather than just painted. These boots are available ready made in a wide range of sizes or made to measure. For custom boots, you can choose from a large selection of toe and heel shapes, stitch designs, boot height and top design, and boot pull shapes. You can also order a matching belt or wallet.

In addition to their fancy dress boots, Lucchese also makes a plain pighide workboot (model 107611) that we find very handsome and, from the looks of it, it ought to wear like iron.

Lucchese is a name to reckon with and, for many people,

has long represented the standard against which other Western boots are measured. Twenty years from now, a pair of Luccheses will have long since earned back their investment price and, if properly cared for, will continue serving you as a prized artifact of American quality craftsmanship.

Available at McCreedy & Schreiber or write Lucchese at 1226 East Houston Street, San Antonio, Texas, 78205 (512) 226-8147 for a local source.

Six examples of Lucchese boots are shown.

6324   Tough water-resistant brown cowhide; Chemi-gum sole. $250.   **(Fig. 6-41)**

6471   French calf. $325.   **(Fig. 6-42)**

6385   Pinfeather ostrich vamp with calf leg. $500.
   (Fig. 6-43)

232O   Lizard vamp with calf leg. $420.   **(Fig. 6-44)**

1445   French calf. $310.   **(Fig. 6-45)**

2083   Domingo goat. $300.   **(Fig. 6-46)**

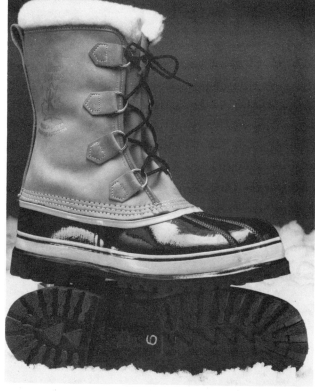

Fig.6-47

Fig.6-48

Sorel pacs, made by the Kaufman Footwear Company of Canada, is one of the most widely respected names in cold weather footgear. The company specializes in boots for wet and freezing conditions. Insulation is provided by a thick felt removable liner, rather like a boot within a boot. Materials and workmanship are top quality. We each have a pair of Sorels and can attest to their excellence. The name Sorel has been consistently recommended to us by professional outdoorspeople and mountaineers who definitely cannot afford to fool around with anything but the best.

Some Sorel models, like the Pathfinder and the Mark X, have yellow label Vibram soles. If you complain of wet, cold feet every winter, then you should seriously consider buying a pair of Kaufmans.

Sorel Aviator over-the-shoe boot: Slips on over your street shoes. Top grain cowhide upper, triple-stitched to rubber vamp. Lined with nylon pile fleece. Full-length heavy-duty zipper. Available from Eddie Bauer. $80.

(Fig. 6-47)

Sorel Caribou: Uppers full grain oil-treated chrome-tanned leather. Bottoms of tough rubber have cleated lug sole. Uppers and bottom cemented together, then triple-stitched. Removable liner of thick felt has genuine shearling collar. Available from Eddie Bauer. $70.   **(Fig. 6-48)**

Fig.6-49

Sorel Renegade: Top of pac is water-repellent heavy-duty nylon bonded to tough rubber bottom. Removable ¼″ thick felt liner. Drawcord at top for snug, snow-free closure. Available from Eddie Bauer. $65. **(Fig. 6-49)**

Sorel Fishawks: Uppers of full grain cowhide triple-stitched to stout rubber bottoms. All stitched seams are la-tex-sealed against leakage. Available from Eddie Bauer and Orvis. $35. **(Fig. 6-50)**

Sorel Mark V: Uppers of full grain oil-treated chrome-tanned leather. Bottoms of tough rubber are mated to up-pers first by cement, then with three rows of heavy stitching protected by a storm welt. Cleated lug soles. Removable felt liner. Available from Eddie Bauer and Holubar. $60. **(Fig. 6-51)**

Sorel Chugalug: Full grain leather upper. Rubber bottom with wraparound crepe rubber sole; wedge heel. Remov-able felt liner has genuine shearling collar. Men's tan; women's white. Available from Eddie Bauer and Holubar. $65. **(Fig. 6-52)**

Fig.6-51

Fig.6-50

Fig.6-52

Red Ball pacs by Uniroyal are high quality, 100% waterproof, durable rubber boots. Built on rocker last for comfort and easy walking. Thick, flexible, tough outsoles and heels, with classic Red Ball hob-nail tread pattern. Uniroyal also makes rubber boots insulated with close cell foam; very good for below freezing conditions. Uniroyal holds a very high reputation for their boot line and is one of the most reliable names around. Beware of low-grade imitations. Available from L. L. Bean.

Red Ball Thermo-ply Calhoun, $49.   **(Fig. 6-53)**

Fig.6-53

Uniroyal also makes a high top wading shoe similar in appearance to a basketball sneaker. Molded rubber lug sole and upper of rubber sandwiched between two layers of nylon. Another good rain shoe. $33.

For more than half a century, the Miller Shoe Company has devoted its entire facilities exclusively to the manufacture of women's low heel comfort shoes, using nine different lasts to ensure proper and comfortable fit for all types of feet. Widely recognized as the best in their field, all Miller "Barefoot Freedom" shoes employ genuine Goodyear welt and all leather construction throughout.

Available nationally at "comfort" shoe stores or for a local source, inquire: Miller Shoe Company, 4015 Cherry Street, Cincinnati, Ohio 45223 (513) 541-1603.

Loveable (5903). $64.	**(Figure 6-54)**
The Alma (899). $62.	**(Figure 6-55)**
Marview (6023), $59.	**(Figure 6-56)**
Tramper (5173). $59.	**(Figure 6-57)**
Fantastic (5974). $58.	**(Figure 6-58)**
Hiker (4316). $59.	**(Figure 6-59)**
Hornet (5902). $58.	**(Figure 6-60)**
Jenny (1921). $62.	**(Figure 6-61)**
Maple (6012). $64.	**(Figure 6-62)**

Fig.6-54

Fig.6-55

Fig.6-56

Fig.6-57

Fig.6-58

Fig.6-59

Fig.6-60

Fig.6-61

Fig.6-62

Fig.6-63

Fig.6-64

In the year 1774, in the small town of Bad Honnef, Johann Adam Birkenstock was registered as a shoemaker. Since that time, the Birkenstock family has been making footwear.

Around the turn of the twentieth century, Herr Conrad Birkenstock originated the revolutionary concept of a contoured insole to conform to the shape of the foot. The name Birkenstock became famous for orthopedic footwear all over the world.

Birkenstock first came to our attention when we began noticing a lot of waiters here in New York wearing them. After hearing constant praise about them from strangers whom we accosted, we decided to try them out ourselves. Sure enough, every syllable of praise was well deserved.

The Birkenstock contoured footbed is made from flexible cork which, after a few wearings, molds itself to the unique shape of your foot. This produces an enormously comfortable shoe which is very lightweight, very flexible, yet provides full support for your feet. Nurses and doctors or anyone who spends a lot of time standing should find them a godsend.

In addition, Birkenstock sells replacement soles so that you can easily resole your shoes yourself. They also sell special innersoles to wear inside your regular shoes which have added greatly to the comfort of some of ours.

Birkenstocks are well-made of high-quality materials. We think the world of them and recommend them highly. Available nationally or for a local source, inquire: Birkenstock, 517-A Jacoby Street, San Rafael, Calif. 94901 (415) 457-4787. For men, women, and children.

The Birkenstock contoured footbed. **(Fig. 6-63)**

A variety of Birkenstock styles for men, women, and children. $35–$70. **(Fig. 6-64)**

Consistently recommended by the people we consulted, Allen Edmonds is one of the finest men's dress shoe manufacturers surviving in America. Workmanship and materials are top-notch. It is the only company of its kind to our knowledge using a shankless construction, where the welted upper and the midsole are stitched together all the way around.

Their prime leathers include such excellent and unusual ones as boarhide, wildebeest, shark, and camel. Shark and wildebeest are exceptionally tough, longwearing, and scuff-resistant.

Available nationally in a broad range of sizes and widths, with most models in a choice of from AAA to EEE. Selected models available from Cable Car, Norm Thompson, and Staffords.

Four examples are shown.

Austin: one piece bal pattern with calfskin uppers. Available from Fellman Shoes. $95. **(Fig. 6-65)**

Viking: genuine boarhide uppers lined with glove leather. Padded ankle collar. Natural crepe rubber soles. $80. **(Fig. 6-66)**

Fig.6-65

Fig.6-66

Wing-tip blucher: sharkskin upper. Full leather calfskin lining. $125.   **(Fig. 6-67)**

Exceptionally durable genuine wildebeest upper. Quarters lined with glove leather; toes lined with cotton twill. Leather insole and midsole. Vibram lug outsole. $85.

(Fig. 6-68)

Fig.6-67

Fig.6-68

Time and again, the brand Nocona has been strongly recommended to us as we sought the names of America's finest Western boot companies. We're satisfied that Nocona ranks right up there among the very top of the list. In conversations with Mr. Joe Justin, vice-president, and Mr. Dale Gordon, sales manager, we were both very impressed by their uncommonly sincere devotion to quality and excellence. Dale Gordon spent two hours patiently explaining the fine points and intricacies of Western boots.

From our own experience with wearing Noconas, we can honestly state that they are unquestionably a first-rate investment at a very fair price. Top-quality Western boots require sophisticated craftsmanship and expertise which just cannot be delivered at a cut-rate price. Nevertheless, for our money, Nocona does a praiseworthy job of keeping the quality way up and the price honest.

Nocona uses an all top-quality leather construction, including sole, stacked leather heel, innersole, and uppers. Their boots are fully leather lined. They have an unusually thick insole, which is the backbone of any quality boot, and a spring steel shank covered with rubber to cushion shock. The heel counter, which helps maintain the boot's shape and support, is also a thick piece of leather that actually curves around underneath the heel.

Nocona does not compromise on quality and is widely recognized in the industry as the premier maker of mass-produced cowboy boots. (Lucchese and Stewart are not really mass manufacturers.) Unlike many Western boots, when it comes time to resole a Nocona, it will not lose its shape because, even with the sole removed, the boot is still structurally intact.

Their line ranges from exotic leathers for dress boots to more hardy everyday boots, using such skins as shark and buffalo as well as cowhide.

Nocona uses a very labor intensive manufacturing process. With the rising price of leather and materials, you'd be well advised to invest now and treat your Noconas well. Available nationally, or for a local source, inquire: Nocona, P.O. Box 599, Nocona, Texas 76255 (817) 825-3321.

Five examples are shown.

Model 9056 Vamps of full quill ostrich hide. Ostrich is considered one of the ideal leathers for comfort and durability. If you own a pair of these, you're a lucky dog and you'd be nuts not to treat them with all due respect. $360. **(Fig. 6-69)**

7900 One of two models available with sharkskin vamp. Shark is exceptionally durable and scuff-resistant. $162. **(Fig. 6-70)**

Fig.6-69

Fig.6-70

Fig.6-71

Fig.6-72

Fig.6-73

5016 Vamp of supple yet durable veal leather. Like all Noconas, it's completely leather lined from top to toe. $124.   **(Fig. 6-71)**

240 One of Nocona's most rugged utility boots with retanned leather vamp and durable synthetic outersole with stout leather midsole. $118.   **(Fig. 6-72)**

181 Steerhide vamp workboot. Built for wear and handsome enough for your next church social. $104. **(Fig. 6-73)**

Here's another of those old-time companies that refuses to knuckle under. We've heard nothing but praise for White's Shoe Shop and in fact another equally excellent boot maker strongly recommended them to us. White's can supply any of their footwear from stock sizes or, for an extra charge, you can have them made up to custom fit.

White's also offers a complete repair and rebuild service for all their footwear and will also repair any make shoe or boot.

For their order booklet showing their full line or to order their shoes, contact: White's Shoe Shop, 430 West Main, Spokane, Wash. 99201 (509) 624-3731.

Three examples are shown.

No. 53 Oxford: hand-sewn construction with high arch and made of dress leather. $140. **(Fig. 6-74)**

No. 690 8″ Packer's Shoe: hand-sewn construction, single heavy oak-tanned leather sole. $126. **(Fig. 6-75)**

No. 375 8″ Smoke Jumper's Boot: heavy oak-tanned leather midsole with Vibram Montagne outsole. Water-repellent all-leather uppers. $145. **(Fig. 6-76)**

Fig.6-74

Fig.6-75

Fig.6-76

Sebago's Hankø Boot is very interesting indeed. The entire upper is made from Krymp Aquaseal leather, a unique water-resistant shrunken oxhide made by the highly respected Aarenes Tannery of Norway. This leather is guaranteed completely waterproof for 4 hours. The waterproofing is permanently sealed into the leather fibers and will not be removed by washing or cleaning. Aarenes also assures us that the leather will remain supple after wettings and won't lose its color. All seams are sealed and the insole is Ensolite foam sandwiched between leather for cushioning and insulation. Available nationally. $75.   **(Fig. 6-77)**

Sebago's Sierra is a very well-constructed, durable desert boot-type shoe. $45.   **(Fig. 6-78)**

The Alden Shoe Company is another of those firms with a superior reputation that the public hears little about.

It is the only high-quality shoe maker we know of still using shell cordovan leather for some of its models.

Alden is widely acknowledged among our consultants as one of the finest men's dress shoe manufacturers to be found. It is one of the principal suppliers of shoes to Brooks Brothers, among others.

In addition to conventional dress shoes, Alden manufactures an excellent line of specialized orthopedic footwear.

For more information, contact: Alden Shoe Co., Taunton St., Middleborough, Mass. 02346 (617) 947-3926.

Four examples are shown.

The Saddle, #997: genuine shell cordovan tip and quarter with scotch grain saddle. Also available with cordovan saddle and other variations.   **(Fig. 6-79)**

Long Wing Tip, #975: shell cordovan upper with double leather sole; reverse storm welt around sole and heel; leather heel with rubber dovetail insert. Also available in imported calfskin.

Plain Toe, #990: Shell cordovan upper; fully leather lined; reverse storm welt around sole and heel. Also available in smooth and grained calfskin.   **(Fig. 6-80)**

Bal Short Wing Tip, #974: shell cordovan upper, fully leather lined; double leather soles; reverse storm welt. Also available in calfskin.   **(Fig. 6-81)**

In certain circles, the words *Lotus Veldtschoen* border on being a mystical incantation. Lotus, among shoe connoisseurs, has a reputation that is almost as bulletproof as the shoes themselves.

We have two pairs of these remarkable specimens and can attest to their prime grade A quality. Given a little care, Lotuses will become one of the "Methuselahs" of your wardrobe. Our friend Don Huxley, former Chief of Clothing for the U.S. Air Force, showed us the pair he was given back in the 1930s and they honestly don't look more than a few years old.

Fig.6-77

Fig.6-78

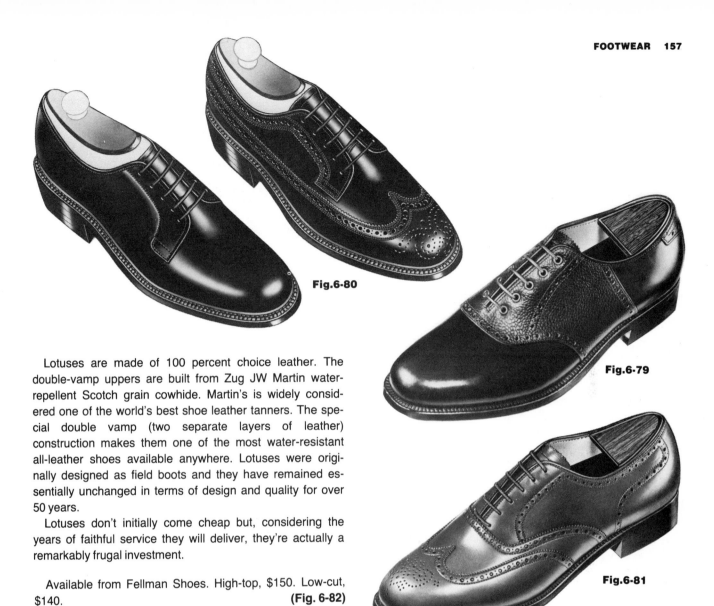

Fig.6-80

Fig.6-79

Fig.6-81

Lotuses are made of 100 percent choice leather. The double-vamp uppers are built from Zug JW Martin water-repellent Scotch grain cowhide. Martin's is widely considered one of the world's best shoe leather tanners. The special double vamp (two separate layers of leather) construction makes them one of the most water-resistant all-leather shoes available anywhere. Lotuses were originally designed as field boots and they have remained essentially unchanged in terms of design and quality for over 50 years.

Lotuses don't initially come cheap but, considering the years of faithful service they will deliver, they're actually a remarkably frugal investment.

Available from Fellman Shoes. High-top, $150. Low-cut, $140. **(Fig. 6-82)**

Fig.6-82

Fig.6-83

Fig.6-84

Fig.6-85

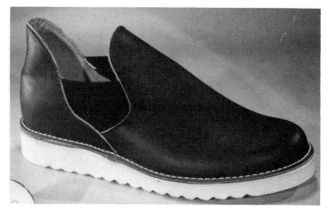

Fig.6-86

Chippewa is one of the country's foremost utility boot and shoe manufacturers. They make footwear using only Goodyear welt construction, which means that all Chippewas can be easily resoled. Most Chippewas are made in a wide range of sizes and widths. Within the shoe industry, their reputation is in high standing. The president of Chippewa told us that his philosophy is to raise the price if necessary rather than cut back on quality. For mass-manufactured utility footwear, Chippewa is just about the best you'll find. Workmanship and materials are first-rate. Selected models are available from Todd's or contact: Chippewa Shoe Co., Chippewa Falls, Wis. 54729 (715) 723-1012 for the name of a dealer near you.

Six examples are shown.

Fig.6-87

Mr. Rugged Junior #6224: oil-tanned upper; Goodyear welt construction with storm welting; leather midsoles. $61. **(Fig. 6-83)**

Vibram Logger #5306: oil-tanned upper; Vibram sole; leather vamp lining. $90. **(Fig. 6-84)**

Modern Suburban #4025: natural rubber midsole; outsole of natural crepe. $59. **(Fig. 6-85)**

The Romeo Work Slipper #4020: This is a very interesting design. Upper of oil-tanned leather; glove cowhide lining; steel shank. $31. **(Fig. 6-86)**

Arctic 50 #5480: Chippewa's extreme cold weather insulated boot with Vibram sole; wool lining; two midsoles, one of sole leather, the other of rubber. $151. **(Fig. 6-87)**

"Choppa" 17″ Safety Biker #7909: leather midsole; leather vamp lining; steel toe. A similar model called the Snaker #3906 is available without steel toes. $105.
(Fig. 6-88)

Elvstrom Sea boots for men and women are lightweight and waterproof, of natural rubber with crepe rubber sole. Reinforced ankle and removable insole. Imported by Canor Plarex. For local source, inquire: Canor Plarex, 4200 Twenty-third Ave. W., Seattle, Wash. 98199 (206) 283-0133. $35. **(Fig. 6-89)**

Fig. 6-88

Fig. 6-89

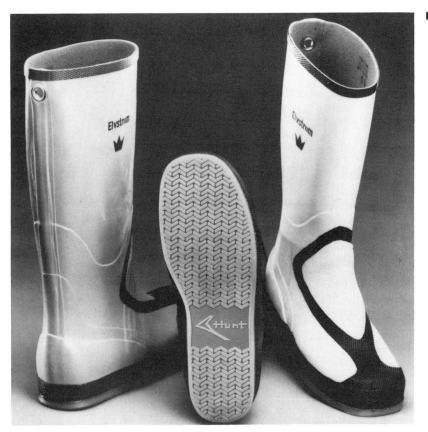

Fig.6-90

Fig.6-91

Fig.6-92

Men's and women's genuine shearling lined slippers with heavy-duty sueded cowhide sole. Hand laced. Available from Orvis. $35.　　　**(Fig. 6-90)**

Dachstein hut slippers, imported from Austria, have leather soles, and 100% oiled wool uppers. Available from Climb High and Sierra Designs. $25.　　　**(Fig. 6-91)**

The Acorn Down Easter slipper sock—the best quality mukluk we've seen. Top grain leather side and sole with a built-in inner sole of close cell comfy foam. Sole stitched to a sock of heavy gray twist in 85% wool, 13% nylon for wear, and 2% spandex. Completely washable.

Constructed with a rocker last for comfortable fit. Not only makes a nice house shoe but great for padding around the backyard. Available from Acorn. $18.50.　　　**(Fig. 6-92)**

We've found that the comfort of many shoes and boots can be increased significantly by slipping in a pair of cushioning insoles. We've tried a lot of brands but the most comfortable insole we've ever encountered is made by Spenco. They're made of closed cell neoprene foam and are exceptionally long-wearing and can be easily washed. $4.50. Available from Eddie Bauer, in sports shops or for a local source, inquire: Spenco Medical Corp., P.O. Box 8113, Waco, Texas 76710 (817) 772-6000.

7

Mail-Order Source Directory

(P) = Pamphlet available
(C) = Catalog available

Acorn Products Company
390 Central Ave.
Lewiston, Maine 04240
(207) 784-9412/9186
deerskin soled slipper socks, handknit
hats and scarves (P)

Eddie Bauer
Fifth and Union
P.O. Box 3700
Seattle, Wash. 98124
(800) 426-8020, 24 hrs.
outdoor haberdashers, down clothing
specialists; unconditional guarantee,
excellent customer service (C)

L. L. Bean
Freeport, Maine 04033
(207) 865-3111, 24 hrs.
outdoor outfitters; unconditional guarantee, excellent customer service (C)

Bergman Company
P.O. Box 56
E. Lempster, N.H. 03605
(603) 863-3646
sweaters (P)

Brigade Quartermaster
P.O. Box 108
Powder Springs, Ga. 30073
(404) 943-9336
surplus and paramilitary clothing and
hardware; 100% satisfaction guaranteed (C)

British Isles Collection
115 Brand Rd.
Salem, Va. 24156
(703) 389-2814
men's and women's haberdashers;
30-day money-back guarantee (C)

I. Buss
738 Broadway
New York, N.Y. 10003
(212) 242-3338
domestic and imported uniform and
surplus clothing

Cable Car Clothiers
150 Post St.
San Francisco, Calif. 94108
(415) 397-7733
men's and women's haberdashers (C)

Cambrian Fly Fishers
5 East 52 St.
New York, N.Y. 10022
(212) 752-4085
outdoor haberdashers; unconditional
lifetime warranty (C)

Carroll and Co.
466 North Rodeo Dr.
Beverly Hills, Calif. 90210
(213) 273-9060
on the chi-chi side but has a high reputation (P)

Casco Bay Trading Post
Freeport, Maine 04032
(207) 865-6371
outdoor clothing; satisfaction guaranteed (C)

Country Store of Concorde
15 Monument St.
Concorde, Mass. 01742
(614) 486-9211
women's haberdashers, some men's
clothing (C)

Danner Shoes
P.O. Box 22204
Portland, Ore. 97222
(503) 653-2920
fine rugged footwear (C)

Dennis Connor
1444 Pioneer Way
El Cajon, Calif. 92020
(714) 440-2324
sailing and casual clothes (C)

Dunham's of Maine
Waterville, Maine 04901
(207) 873-6165
fine men's and women's clothing; satisfaction guaranteed (C)

Early Winters Ltd.
110 Prefontaine Pl. S.
Seattle, Wash. 98104
(206) 622-5203
outdoor equippers; 30-day money-
back guarantee; lifetime warranty
against defects (C)

Eastern Mountain Sports, Inc.
Vose Farm Rd.
Peterborough, N.H. 03458
(603) 924-9212, 24 hrs.
outdoor equippers; unconditional guarantee (C)

Fellman Shoes
12 East 46 St./24 East 44 St.
New York, N.Y. 10017
(212) 682-3144
American importers of Lotus Veldt-
schoens, other fine footwear (P)

C. C. Filson
205 Maritime Bldg.
Seattle, Wash. 98104
(206) 624-4437
fine rugged outdoor clothing; satisfaction guaranteed (P)

Flight Suits Ltd.
1050 J Pioneer Way
El Cajon, Calif. 92020
(714) 448-8959
custom aeronautical clothiers and
automobile racing wear; unconditional
guarantee or money back (P)

French Creek Sheep and Wool Co.
Elverson, Pa. 19520
(215) 286-5700
superb shearling coats, natural oiled wool sweaters, and other fine men's and women's clothing; 14-day refund or exchange for any reason, unconditional lifetime guarantee against defects (C)

Gander Mountain
P.O. Box 248
Wilmot, Wis. 53192
(800) 558-9410
general outdoor outfitters (C)

Gokeys
P.O. Box 43659/84
South Wabasha St.
St. Paul, Minn. 55107
(612) 292-3911, 24 hrs.
men's and women's haberdashers; satisfaction guaranteed (C)

Great Pacific Ironworks
P.O. Box 150
Ventura, Calif. 93001
(800) 235-3371
rugged outdoor clothes and climbing regalia; satisfaction guaranteed (C)

Harborside Shop
Bay View St.
Camden, Maine 04843
(207) 236-4567
outdoor clothiers; satisfaction guaranteed (P)

Holubar Mountaineering Ltd.
P.O. Box 7
Boulder, Colo. 80306
(800) 525-2540
outdoor equippers, down clothing; complete satisfaction guaranteed (C)

International Mountain Equipment
P.O. Box 494/Main St.
North Conway, N.H. 03860
(603) 356-5287
outdoor equippers and climbing regalia; complete satisfaction guaranteed, very knowledgeable staff (C)

Kalpakian Knitting Mills
605 West Eighth Ave.
Vancouver, B.C. V5Z 1C 7
(604) 873-4717
virgin wool sweaters and socks; 21-day money-back guarantee (P)

Komito Boots
P.O. Box 2106
Estes Park, Colo. 80517
(303) 586-5391
mountain footwear specialists, expert boot repair service; satisfaction assured, guarantee against defects (P)

Kreeger & Son
16 West 46 St.
New York, N.Y. 10036
(212) 575-7825
outdoor outfitters; satisfaction guaranteed (P)

Land's End
105 Leffler St.
Dodgeville, Wis. 53533
(800) 356-2931
sailing and casual clothes (C)

Peter Limmer & Sons, Inc.
Intervale, N.H. 03845
(603) 356-5378
superb hiking boots, custom-made and stock sizes; complete satisfaction guaranteed (P)

Lowe Alpine Systems
P.O. Box 189
Lafayette, Colo. 80026
(800) 525-2945
mountaineering clothes and equipment; 10-day money-back guarantee, unconditional lifetime guarantee against defects (P)

Marmot Mountain Works
331 South 13 St.
Grand Junction, Colo. 81501
(800) 525-7070
down clothing specialists and outdoor clothing; 30-day money-back satisfaction guaranteed, lifetime warranty against defects (C)

McCreedy & Schreiber
37 West 46 St./55 West 46 St.
New York, N.Y. 10036
(212) 582-1552
Lucchese boots and other fine footwear (P)

Randal Merrell
228 South 1500 West
Vernal, Utah 84078
(801) 789-3079
superb custom-made handcrafted hiking and Western boots; complete satisfaction guaranteed (P)

Moor and Mountain
63 Park St.
Andover, Mass. 01810
(617) 475-3665
outdoor outfitters; 14-day money-back refund, unconditional guarantee against defects (C)

David Morgan
P.O. Box 70190
Seattle, Wash. 98107
(206) 282-3300
rustic durable clothing; satisfaction guaranteed (C)

Norm Thompson
P.O. Box 3999
Portland, Ore. 97208
(800) 547-1160/1532
men's and women's haberdashers; lifetime satisfaction guaranteed (C)

Orvis
Manchester, Vt. 05254
(802) 362-1300
outdoor haberdasher; 100% satisfaction guaranteed (C)

REI (Recreational Equipment Inc.)
P.O. Box C-88125
Seattle, Wash. 98188
(800) 426-4840
outdoor equippers; complete satisfaction guaranteed (C)

Robbins Mountaingear/ Mountainwear
Box 4536
Modesto, Calif. 95352
(209) 529-6913
sweaters and mountaineering clothes; unconditional lifetime warranty against defects (C)

Rugged Wear Ltd.
Narragansett, R.I. 02882
(401) 789-4115
excellent rugby shirts, shorts, and trousers (P)

W. C. Russell
285 Southwest Franklin
Berlin, Wis. 54923
(414) 361-2252
excellent handcrafted moccasins, boots, and shoes, custom and stock sizes; satisfaction guaranteed (C)

Sierra Designs
247 Fourth St.
Oakland, Calif. 94607
(800) 227-1120
outdoor clothiers; satisfaction guaranteed (C)

The Ski Hut
P.O. Box 309/1615 University Ave.
Berkeley, Calif. 94701
(415) 843-8170
outdoor clothiers; satisfaction guaranteed (C)

Milt Spark's Belts
P.O. Box 7
Idaho City, Idaho 83631
(208) 392-6695
superlative rugged belts and other firearm leather goods (P)

Split-S Aviation
1050 J Pioneer Way
El Cajon, Calif. 92020
(714) 440-0894
leather flight wear; satisfaction guaranteed (C)

Staffords
P.O. Box 2055/808 Smith Ave.
Thomasville, Ga. 31792
(912) 226-4306
outdoor haberdashers; complete satisfaction guaranteed (C)

Talbots
164 North St.
Hingham, Mass. 02043
(617) 749-7830
women's haberdashers, some men's; satisfaction guaranteed (C)

Todd's
5 South Wabash Ave.
Chicago, Ill. 60603
(312) 372-1335
Chippewa footwear; satisfaction and fit guaranteed (P)

U.S. Cavalry Store
1375 North Wilson Rd.
Radcliff, Ky. 40160
(502) 351-1164
military clothing and accessories (C)

White's Shoes
430 West Main
Spokane, Wash. 99201
(509) 624-3731
fine rugged boots and shoes (P)

Whole Earth Provisions Co.
2410 San Antonio St.
Austin, Tex. 78705
(512) 478-1577
outdoor clothing; 10-day money-back guarantee (C)

PART THREE

MATERIALS AND MAINTENANCE

8

Anatomy of a Fabric

YARNS AND WEAVES

The basic properties of a textile fabric depend to a large extent on those of the fiber from which it is made. (For Fiber Characteristics see page 172. The general properties and performance of a fabric can be considerably altered, however, by modifications in the spinning and in the weaving or knitting process, as well as by finishes.

Woven fabrics are produced by interlacing one yarn (or thread) with another at right angles. The yarns that are put down on the loom first and which determine the length of the fabric, are called the *warp* yarns. These run parallel to the selvedge. The yarns that go over and under the warp yarns are called the *filling* yarns. Other terms used in the trade are *picks* (filling yarns) and *ends* (warp yarns).

Generally, warp yarns are stronger and closer together than the filling yarns because they must be held under tension and are subjected to greater strains during weaving. Filling yarns are under little tension and therefore need not be as strong. This is why, when fabrics shrink, they tend to shrink more in the direction of the lengthwise grain; laundering relaxes the yarns back to their original dimensions.

The yarns that go into the fabric may be one- or multi-ply and have varying degrees of twist. Multi-ply yarns are two or more yarns twisted together into a single yarn; they are stronger than one-ply yarns.

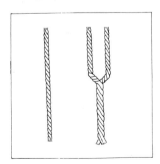

Single- and two-ply yarn

The more you twist a yarn, the stronger and finer it will become, at least up to a certain point. It will also become more elastic. If you twist it to the point that it starts to kink, you are creating a crepe yarn. Creped yarns are relatively weak, and fabrics made of these highly twisted yarns have a greater tendency to shrink and stretch.

Loosely twisted yarns can be used to create fluffy, fleecy surfaces; tightly twisted yarns produce a smooth, more even surface. If filament yarns of a high luster are given a low twist, they will reflect greater quantities of light and appear brighter than the same yarn more tightly twisted.

High twist yarns, providing they are not twisted to the kinking point, are generally stronger and are also much more abrasion resistant. The fibers in a low twist yarn can easily snag or pull up. High twist yarns tend to shed soil more easily. Because their surface is smoother, there are fewer fiber ends to attract and hold soil. Absorbency is somewhat reduced. A fabric made with high twist yarns and having a smooth surface, such as a serge, will generally show less signs of wear than a softer, fluffier fabric made with less highly twisted yarns.

Cotton yarn that is spun from the shorter, more irregular fibers of the cotton is called *carded* yarn. Cotton yarn made from the longer fibers remaining after the shorter fibers have been combed out and removed is called *combed cotton* yarn. This is a finer, smoother, and generally stronger yarn.

Wool yarns may also be made from longer or shorter fibers. Shorter fibers are used to make a soft yarn called *woolen.* Examples of woolen fabrics are flannel and tweed. Long wool fibers spun parallel are used to make a smooth, highly twisted yarn called *worsted,* which is made into gabardine, cavalry twill, and serge, for example.

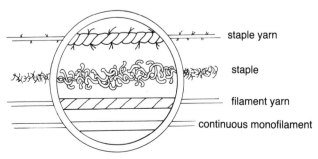

Types of yarn

Yarns spun from shorter staple lengths are more irregular than those spun from the much longer filament fibers. The short ends of the fiber, projecting from the yarn surface, produce a fuzzy effect. Spun yarns are also more bulky than filament yarns of the same weight and are therefore often used to make porous, warm fabrics. Unfortunately, the fuzz on the yarn wears off quite easily, resulting in worn spots or bald patches in the fabric.

Filament yarns, made from the much longer uncut man-made or silk filaments, do not need to be twisted. Their smooth surface results in lustrous fabrics. They have an almost slick feel or "hand," tend to shed dirt and lint, resist pilling, and are usually quite strong. They also tend to snag more easily, however.

Filament yarns can also be specially treated to give them texture, simulating some of the characteristics of spun yarn fabrics.

There are three basic types of weaves and endless variations on them. The plain weave is the simplest, where each filling yarn is interlaced over one and under one warp yarn. If closely woven, it can be firm and strong, like sheeting, or it can be a very loose weave, like cheesecloth. Firm constructions wear well, seldom ravel, but show wrinkles easily and can have poor tear strength.

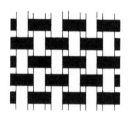

Plain weave

Two common variations on the plain weave are the rib and the basket weaves. Ribbed, or corded, fabrics are created by using a larger yarn in one direction. Broadcloth and poplin are examples. Rib fabrics may wear unevenly, because crossing over the larger yarns exposes a greater area of the covering yarn to abrasion. For best durability, the crossing yarns should be closely spaced and have a good twist, and the ribs should not be too pronounced.

The basket weave combines two or more warp and/or two or more filling yarns as a single yarn. Hopsacking and oxford cloth are common examples. The basket variation cannot be woven as tightly as a plain weave so it stretches easily and may shrink when washed. Also, the yarns have a tendency to slip out of place.

In the twill weave, the filling yarn goes over two or more of the warp yarns, then under one or more of the warp yarns. In each successive row, the sequence begins one yarn to the right or left. Twill weaves can be readily identified by the diagonal ridges on the surface. The yarns are usually packed tightly together and held firmly in place, making a strong, durable weave that is heavier and sturdier than a plain weave and has good abrasion resistance. The

compact structure of the weave allows it to shed dirt more easily, although when soiled, twills can sometimes be more difficult to clean because of their uneven surface. Twills include gabardine, denim, tweed, serge, flannel, and whipcord.

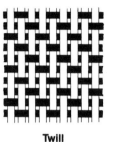

Twill

One common variation is the herringbone twill, where the direction of the twill reverses itself to form a broken diagonal that appears like a series of V's.

In the satin weave, yarns are "floated" over 4 or as many as 12 yarns before interlacing. These floats catch the light, giving a satin weave its lustrous appearance and its smooth, slippery surface that tends to shed dirt easily. However, long floats are also more subject to abrasion and snagging. The more densely woven the weave, the more durable it will be.

Satin weave

KNITS

Knit fabrics stretch and conform to the body because the yarns are freer to move within the loop construction and the loops can lengthen or widen to give stretch in either direction. For the same reason, they are also less stable and require careful handling in washing to prevent excessive shrinking or misshaping.

Jersey knit is just a mechanized version of hand knitting. It is simple, quick to produce, relatively inexpensive, and therefore very common. Jersey knits show a smooth, flat

face

back

Jersey knit

face of vertical lines and horizontal rows of V's on the reverse side. It stretches equally in both directions. Jersey is less stable than some other knits; has a tendency to curl at the edges; and, if a yarn is broken, it will run.

Interlock looks the same on both sides and resembles the face side of a jersey knit. In fact, it is much as though two pieces of jersey were knitted together, or interlocked, during construction. The resulting material is firmer, thicker, and also more stable. It does not ravel, is resistant to runs, and will not curl up at the edges.

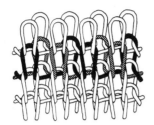

Interlock

Doubleknits are constructed using the interlock stitch and variations of it that allow decorative patterns to be knitted in. Doubleknits have received a bad name from some of the uses to which they have been put, but there is nothing wrong with the fabric construction itself. Doubleknits are made not just of polyester but also of fine wools or any other fiber.

Tricot employs a different knitting method known as warp knit. (The above mentioned knits are all weft knitting.) Warp knits have little crosswise stretch and do not run or ravel because loops are interlocked from side to side as well as vertically. Warp knitting is the fastest method for making cloth and produces a material with fine vertical rows on the face and crosswise ribs on the back. Tricot is produced on a warp knitting machine using a plain jersey stitch. Like jersey, it will curl at the edges but is run- and ravel-proof, has high tear strength, and good stability, resiliency, and elasticity.

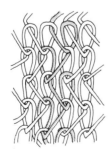

Single-warp tricot knit

BLENDS

It is sometimes desirable to blend two or more different fibers into one fabric. Frequently, man-made fibers are blended with natural fibers in order to take advantage of the best qualities of each. In other cases, a relatively cheap fiber may be blended with a more expensive one either to keep down the cost or for prestige value. For example, a small quantity of cashmere might be blended with sheep's wool.

The blends that concern us here are those designed to combine improved performance and appearance. In theory, blends should bring to the fabric the best advantages of each fiber included in the blend. For example, a cotton/polyester fabric should combine polyester's wrinkle resistance and durability with cotton's absorbency and washability. In actuality, what is achieved is more of a compromise.

On the whole, a fabric must contain at least 15 to 20 percent of any given fiber for that fiber to make any worthwhile contribution to the fabric's performance, *except* in the case of such fibers as spandex or rubber.

In intimate blends, the different fibers are blended together into a single yarn, which is then woven into fabric. In engineered blends, yarns of different fibers are woven into one fabric. For example, the warp of an engineered blend may be a polyester yarn, the filling a cotton yarn. The potential disadvantage to this type of blend is that if the cotton shrinks and the polyester does not, this could well cause distortion in the fabric and the garment shape. This would not happen with an intimate blend. Unfortunately, labels do not presently specify what type of blend the fabric is.

Pilling is frequently a nasty problem with a blend of natural and man-made fibers. Pills are small balls of fiber that have broken off from a yarn but still cling to the surface of the fabric. All fabrics pill to some degree but this is seldom troublesome with natural fabrics because the pills are easily brushed off or fall off by themselves. In blends, the superior strength of the man-made fibers prevents the pill from coming off, making the garment look chintzy and ugly. This problem of pilling in natural/man-made blends is much more severe with softer, nappier fabrics than it is with harder, tightly woven ones.

FINISHES

Resin finishes can make fabrics shrink resistant, wrinkle resistant, or soil and water resistant. Unfortunately, these finishes are somewhat damaging to fibers and will reduce the fabric's moisture absorption, abrasion resistance, and durability.

Durable press (also known as permanent press) treated fabrics require little or no ironing, have improved wrinkle resistance, are stabilized against shrinkage, and creases can be durably set in. This finish is indeed durable but will not always last the lifespan of the garment. It is a somewhat expensive process and special care must be taken during garment manufacture to ensure good results.

Unfortunately, durable press treated fabrics suffer some

loss of strength and their abrasion resistance is reduced. Polyester is commonly blended into a durable press fabric to compensate somewhat for this. Collars and cuffs, knees and elbows, and the edges of sharp creases become more easily worn and frayed because the resin treatment actually embrittles cotton fabric. In addition, durable press requires special laundering and oil-borne stains in particular are difficult to launder out. Soil release finishes have been developed to counteract this problem.

All-cotton Sanforset treated clothes require a little more ironing than do all-man-made fabrics or blends but are more absorbent (although their absorbency is less than untreated cottons), release oily soils more readily, and have fewer problems of pilling and static build-up. They need to be a relatively heavier weight than do blends in order to accept the resin.

Durable press garments must be bought to fit because, once creases and pleats are set in, alterations can become difficult. For example, if you need to lengthen a hem, the original crease line will always show. Also, when the hem is shortened, it may prove difficult to achieve as sharp a crease as the manufacturer provided.

Soil release finishes were developed largely in response to the tendency of durable press to hold oily stains. Some work by preventing oil and dirt from penetrating the fabric; others by improving the ability of laundering to remove soil and stains. Unfortunately, they have a limited lifespan.

Many water-repellent finishes, such as Scotchgard and Zepel, also make fabrics spot and stain resistant. These resist penetration by water but are not waterproof. Renewable water repellent finishes must be reapplied after each laundering or dry cleaning. Durable finishes have a much longer life expectancy but may be durable either only to laundering or only to dry cleaning, so care labels should be carefully followed.

FIBER CHARACTERISTICS

There is a great deal of controversy over natural versus man-made fibers, each opposing side extolling the virtues of its own preference to the detriment of the other. The origins of this controversy stem from special interest groups within the textile industry who, in the interests of promoting their own particular product, emphasize their competitor's weak points, frequently exaggerating these weaknesses to the point of scare stories.

Although much research and testing has been undertaken to prove the commonly held notion that natural fibers are "more comfortable" than man-made ones, no definite scientific evidence has proven that this is true. Each fiber can be a good choice for the proper end use. Just as when only natural fibers were available, each was considered best for certain purposes, so now, even when the choice is so much greater, the same still holds true.

Regrettably, wool, cotton, and flax all require a great deal of agricultural land. Long-term priorities will have to be carefully weighed for using this limited land for growing food or fiber. The economics are such that natural fibers, especially wool, may soon become luxury items. Consider the fact that a single manufacturing plant on 300 acres produces as much weight of polyester fiber as the weight of cotton grown on 600,000 acres. It is certainly in your interests to invest now in high-quality, preferably long staple, wools and cottons.

NATURAL FIBERS

Cotton and Linen

Cotton and linen are both cellulosic fibers and have certain common characteristics. They are both very comfortable to wear. Because they have high absorbency, they absorb and transmit body moisture, keeping you feeling dry. For the same reason, they also are slow to dry, dye very well, and do not build up static electricity. They wrinkle easily, however, and the wrinkles do not readily hang out because the fiber's elasticity and resilience is poor. However, wrinkles can be easily pressed out and pleats and sharp creases pressed in.

Aside from their wrinkling problem, these materials are easy to care for because they can withstand high washing and drying temperatures, strong detergents, and moderate bleaching. They are in fact about 20 percent stronger when wet. They will, however, shrink unless they have been specially treated. Few insects like these fibers, although silverfish enjoy the starch in starched fabrics. Damp materials will mildew and prolonged exposure to sunlight damages the fibers.

Cotton and linen can both be mercerized. Mercerization is a process using a strong caustic solution which produces intensive permanent swelling of the fibers, resulting in greatly increased luster and dying qualities, increased capacity to absorb water vapor from the ambient air, and increased strength of as much as 20 percent.

Cotton can be woven either into very fine, smooth fabrics using long staple fibers or into heavy, coarse fabrics using short staple fibers. It can also make fluffy materials such as flannelette and thick cellular fabrics such as insulated underwear materials.

Egyptian, Sea Island, pima, and supima are all long staple cottons that can be woven into thin, smooth, almost silky fabrics. These are regarded as the best quality cottons. They are in relatively short supply because they are difficult to grow and much slower to mature, providing greater opportunity for attacks by weevils and other insects.

Long staple cotton fibers range in length from $1\frac{1}{8}''$ to approximately $2\frac{1}{2}''$, whereas the shorter staple variety can be as little as $\frac{1}{4}''$ long.

Flax, used to make linen, is a much longer staple fiber

than cotton, ranging from 6″ to over 20″ in length. Therefore fabrics made of flax are usually smoother than cotton because longer fiber lengths result in fewer fiber ends in the yarn. Smoothness makes it more resistant to the adhesion of dirt. It is stronger and more lustrous than cotton but somewhat less resilient, and therefore wrinkles more easily.

Linen is in quite short supply and tends to be rather expensive. It represents only 3 percent of the total world fiber production, with most flax being grown in East and West Europe. No flax is grown in the United States. No fabric may be labeled "linen" or "pure flax" or carry a name implying it is linen unless the fabric is in fact made of 100 percent linen.

Wool and Silk

Wool and silk are both protein fibers. These have better resilience than cellulosic fibers and are therefore more resistant to wrinkling and hold their shape well. Fabrics made from these fibers also tend to feel lighter in weight than comparable cellulosic fabrics. Protein fibers do not burn easily and, when set aflame, generally will self-extinguish quickly once the flame source has been removed.

Both should be ironed at a relatively low temperature and, because dry heat may damage them, always use steam or a press cloth. Silk may water-spot. Wool tends to be weaker than cotton and linen and, because it is even weaker wet than dry, it must be handled with great care when hand washed. Silk, being a filament fiber, is stronger than cotton and linen.

Never use chlorine bleach on protein fibers (wool, silk, and down); it will damage them and cause yellowing. Strongly alkaline soaps and detergents should also be avoided, but hydrogen peroxide can safely be used.

Sunlight may yellow white fabrics. Although wool has better resistance to sunlight than cotton, it will degrade on prolonged exposure and silk degrades quite easily. Clothes moths and carpet beetles love protein fibers.

Wool

Compared with many other fibers, wool is relatively weak but its resilience, elongation, and elastic recovery nevertheless make it a very desirable clothing fabric. Wool has a unique natural crimp, so it can be stretched from two to nine times its relaxed length without breaking and can be bent back and forth without breaking 20,000 times, as opposed to 3,000 for cotton. Fine wools have 20 to 30 crimps per inch and can therefore stretch far more than a coarse wool, which may have only two crimps to the inch. Because of this unique characteristic, wool fabrics will readily spring back into shape after crushing and creasing.

Roughly 80 percent of the total fabric volume of woolens is air, making them potentially a very good insulator. Another reason wool feels warm is that only tiny sections or ends of the wool fiber come into direct contact with one's skin; these ends are so rapidly warmed by body heat that there is practically no sensation of heat loss.

Each fiber is covered by a thin, water-repellent sheath called the epicuticle. This makes wool somewhat water resistant but, in practical daily wear applications, wool will get wet just as easily in rain as any other material. Once saturated, it will lose much of its insulative value and, contrary to folk wisdom and advertising malarkey, wool when wet will not give off heat to keep you warm. Wool has a higher moisture absorbency than *any* other textile fiber (including cotton and linen) and moisture is absorbed and held *inside* the fiber, not on the surface. So wool feels relatively dry even on a humid day. This absorbency of wool also allows dyes to penetrate deeply into the fibers.

The quality of wool varies with the breed of the sheep and also depends on which part of the sheep it was taken from. Australian and New Zealand wools are considered among the best, as is wool from the Merino sheep, which produces a very long, fine strand wool. True Shetland wool is relatively short and coarse. However, the name has never been trademarked or copyrighted and is therefore used very loosely.

Even though wool requires dry cleaning or extremely careful hand washing, it is relatively easy to keep clean. Because of its moisture content, it is relatively free of static electricity which attracts dirt and lint; spills run off and surface dirt can also be easily brushed off. Wrinkles generally hang out overnight.

Wool must be treated very carefully in hand washing; it is very sensitive to alkalies and the thin epicuticle sheath is easily damaged by rough handling and scrubbing. Once damaged, the wool then becomes much easier to saturate. This scaly sheath also gives rise to felting when subjected to rough handling when wet. This characteristic is used to advantage in the making of felt or melton cloth, but it is obviously not something you want to happen to your clothes. Machine-washable wools have been chemically treated to prevent felting and should be washed according to the care label.

Wool must be protected against moths and carpet beetles whose larvae adore the wool protein as food. Some wools are moth-proofed at the manufacturing stage but, due to the cost of the process, this is rare. Wool clothes should be specially stored during the summer (see page 187).

Wool Labeling

The WOOLMARK is assigned by the Wool Bureau, Inc. to apparel products of pure virgin wool that meet internationally enforced standards of quality.

The WOOLBLEND mark is assigned by the Wool Bureau, Inc. for the promotion of products containing wool combined with other fibers, synthetic or natural, based on a minimum of 60 percent wool as a blend level or the requirements of the product.

Wool fabrics can be made from new or from used wool but one cannot always tell the difference just by looking at the fabric. The Wool Products Labeling Act regulates the labeling of sheep's wool and other animal hair fibers. The provisions of this act are as follows:

All wool products must be labeled.

Fibers contained in the product, except for ornamentation, must be identified.

The following terms are defined by statute:

Wool: ". . . the fiber from the fleece of the sheep or lamb or hair of the Angora or Cashmere goat (and may include the so-called specialty fibers from the hair of the camel, alpaca, llama, and vicuna) which has never been reclaimed from any woven or felted wool product."

Reprocessed wool: "The resulting fiber when wool has been woven or felted into a wool product which, without ever having been utilized in any way by the ultimate consumer, subsequently has been made into a fibrous state." This would include wools reprocessed from cutting scraps.

Reused wool: "The resulting fiber when wool or reprocessed wool has been spun, woven, knitted, or felted into a wool product which, after having been used in any way by the ultimate consumer, subsequently is made into a fibrous state."

The terms *new wool* or *virgin wool* may be used "only when the product or part (of a product) referred to is composed wholly of new or virgin fibers which has [sic] never been reclaimed from any spun, woven, knitted, felted, bonded, or similarly manufactured product."

Reprocessed wools are often made from the cutting scraps left from the manufacture of wool products. In the process of pulling apart the fibers and returning them to the fibrous state, fibers may be damaged and may therefore be lower in quality than some new wool. Reused wool is the lowest quality because the wool as a product has been subjected to normal wear and tear by the consumer and then may sustain further damage when it is reconverted to its fibrous state. Reused wools are often made into interlinings for jackets and coats. The terms *virgin* or *new* wool in themselves, carry no guarantee of *quality*. It is possible that a poor quality virgin wool may be inferior to an excellent quality reprocessed wool.

Specialty Wools

Alpaca: The domesticated alpaca, a relative of the llama, is sheared once every two years for its strong, glossy fibers. Hairs average 8″ to 12″ in length and colors range from white to brown to black. The alpaca is native to Peru, Bolivia, Ecuador, and Argentina.

Cashmere: Cashmere fiber is obtained from the fleece of the Cashmere (or Kashmir) goat. It is gathered by combing hairs from the fleece of the domesticated animal during the shedding season. The natural colors are gray, brown, and occasionally white. Cashmere is finer than sheep's wool and more easily damaged by alka-

lies. In fact, the fiber is so fine that it takes about two miles of yarn, or the fleeces of three goats, to make one average-size man's pullover. The fiber abrades easily because of its softness and, because fabrics are often constructed with a napped or fleecy surface, they require careful handling. The softness and luster of cashmere, combined with its scarcity, makes it an expensive luxury fiber. It feels wonderful but offers poor durability.

Camel Hair: This fiber comes only from the two hump Bactrian camel of Central Asia, not from the Mid-Eastern one hump dromedary. In the spring, when the weather starts to get warm, the camels begin to shed. Specially assigned people with baskets follow the camel caravans as they move from place to place and collect the hair as it drops to the ground. It is estimated one camel produces from 5 to 8 pounds of hair each year.

Camel hair is light brown or tan in color. Because this color cannot be bleached out, camel fabrics are left in their natural color or dyed to darker shades.

Camel hair provides excellent warmth with little weight and it is expensive. It is also relatively weak, easily damaged by abrasion because of its softness, and soon tends to show signs of wear. Because sheep wool can be easily dyed a camel color and blended with a little camel hair, there may be misrepresentation of the final product as "camel hair" when in fact there is very little, if any, camel hair in it.

Llama: The domesticated llama, native to the Andes, produces a fine, lustrous fleece similar to alpaca, although slightly weaker. Predominant colors are black and brown.

Mohair: The United States is the principal producer of mohair. Mohair is clipped from the mohair or angora goat, which can produce from 5 to 7 pounds of hair a year. (The angora rabbit produces a very fine, slippery, hard-to-spin fiber.) Mohair has a very high luster and a slippery smooth surface. Especially resistant to abrasion and wear, it is easier to launder and neither shrinks nor felts as easily as sheep's wool. Quality can vary a good deal. The finest mohair, known as "kid mohair," is obtained from the young goat. The fiber from mature animals is coarser and less suitable for clothing fabrics.

Silk

Silk is a continuous protein filament that can be as much as a mile long. The silkworm caterpillar spins the silk from a tiny opening in its mouth, called a spinneret, to form a cocoon of silk around itself preparatory to metamorphosing into a chrysalis and then a moth. The cocoons, when cultivated commercially, are treated with heat to kill the moth chrysalis inside; if the moth was allowed to hatch, it would break through the cocoon and thus break the silk filament. Wild moths, of course, hatch out, breaking their cocoons, which is why wild silk filaments are shorter and irregular in length.

The silk filament is then very carefully unwound by hand from the cocoon. Most of the finest silk comes from Japan, where the science of sericulture, or silkworm culture, has been carefully developed.

Silk has a warm soft, rich luster. Cultivated silk is off-white to cream color; wild silk is brown, and both dye readily with beautiful brilliant colors. It is one of the strongest natural fibers in relation to its filament fineness, although it is slightly weaker when wet, thus requiring careful handling during washing.

Good absorption, moderate elasticity, and resilience, are all characteristics of silk. Creases will hang out, although silk's wrinkle recovery is slower and not as good as wool's. Densely woven fabrics can be quite warm or silk can be woven into sheer, lightweight fabrics suitable for summer clothing.

Silk tends to build up static electricity, which can attract dust and lint but being a filament fiber with few loose ends, it sheds dust and dirt readily.

In cleaning, silk does not tend to stretch or shrink to any significant extent, it gives up soil readily, and dries quickly. However, perspiration will cause deterioration of the fabric and can discolor dyes. Carpet beetles will attack the fiber and silk is also particularly susceptible to damage from strong light.

Silk production is very limited; it is an expensive fiber that requires delicate handling in cleaning. Chlorine bleach should never be used.

MAN-MADE FIBERS

Most man-made fibers including the cellulosics are produced by forcing or extruding a syrupy substance through the tiny holes of a spinneret, thus forming a continuous filament of the desired length.

The spinneret, similar in principle to a shower head, can have from one to thousands of tiny holes. Once the liquid is forced through the holes, the emerging filaments are then hardened or solidified.

Because man-made fibers are extruded, they can be formed in various thicknesses, or deniers, from a 15 denier yarn for fine hosiery to 840 denier for truck tires. The long filaments, if desired, can be cut into short staple lengths to more closely resemble the look and feel of natural fibers.

Cellulosic Fibers

Rayon, acetate, and triacetate, unlike other man-made fibers, are produced from a cellulosic base, such as wood pulp.

Rayon was the first man-made fiber, produced commercially in 1911, when it was called artificial silk.

Rayon, also known as viscose, is sometimes presented as a competitor to cotton. But rayons stretch and shrink more than cotton, have extremely poor abrasion resistance, and lose strength when wet. They are even more absorbent than cotton and accept dye readily. They are soft and drape well. Like cotton, rayons are subject to damage from mildew, silverfish, and exposure to sunlight. Dry cleaning is advised or wash with extreme care, because rayon shrinks severely.

High wet modulus rayon was developed to possess more of the properties of cotton. It has increased strength, better resilience and elasticity, less tendency to stretch or shrink, can tolerate higher ironing temperatures, and resists sunlight better. Its absorbency is decreased, however, which also makes it somewhat more difficult to dye, although still relatively easy compared with many man-made fibers. High wet modulus is not significantly better than viscose rayon.

Also, rayon is a relatively expensive fiber.

Acetate and *triacetate* both have very low strength and are weaker wet than dry. Abrasion resistance, although slightly better than rayon's, is so poor that just nylon hosiery rubbing against an acetate satin lining in a coat will abrade the lining. Both have low absorbency, especially triacetate, and both tend to build up static electricity. Consequently, these fibers may not feel as cool to wear as cotton, linen, or rayon.

Acetate has poor wrinkle resistance and elastic recovery and tends to shrink with laundering and high temperatures.

In contrast, triacetate is resilient and has good wrinkle recovery, as well as good resistance to stretching and shrinking.

Most acetate garments should be dry cleaned, although careful hand laundering can be acceptable. Triacetates can be hand- or machine-washed or dry cleaned.

Acetone, found in nail polish remover and some perfumes, will damage or dissolve acetate and triacetate.

SYNTHETIC FIBERS

Although each of the synthetic or petroleum base fibers has many individual qualities, these fibers as a class possess some common properties.

Most have good abrasion resistance and good resilience, allowing them to spring back when crushed and stay relatively wrinkle-free.

They tend to be sensitive to heat; however, this allows pleats, creases, and other special features to be permanently heat-set into the fabric. They tend to be hydrophobic or water-resistant; this lower absorbency may lead to a decrease in comfort when synthetics are worn next to the skin in warm temperatures. Equally, synthetics dry quickly after laundering. Low absorbency can create difficulties in dying and in the penetration of dyes. You will sometimes see paler areas at elbows, knees, and other points of wear where the dye has rubbed off the surface, exposing the undyed fiber beneath. This is known as "frosting" and is the sign of a poor dying job. With today's modern advances in dying, there is no excuse for frosting to occur. Low absorbency also allows static electricity build-up, which attracts dirt and lint and causes static cling and shocks.

Synthetics are also oleophilic or oil-absorbing. Oil and grease stains can be difficult to remove and stain removal is made additionally difficult by their low water absorbency. Once the soil has penetrated the fiber, the fiber's resistance to water interferes with soil removal during laundering or cleaning. However, low absorbency makes them initially quite resistant to water-borne soil and stains.

Many man-made fibers are rather smooth and slippery to the touch, which causes some problems in sewing in order to keep seams from pulling out when sudden stress is applied. This can be somewhat reduced by special texturizing during the manufacturing process.

Man-mades have a particular tendency to pill. All fabrics pill to some degree but, on natural fibers, the tangled ends wear off or can be pulled off, whereas pills on synthetic fibers cling tenaciously. When man-mades and naturals are blended together, this pilling problem is aggravated.

Synthetics resist insects, mildew, and bacterial growth. Any insect will eat food spots and stains, however, and in the course of doing so, eat the fiber as well. So be careful to store clothes in a clean condition.

Nylon

Nylon has excellent strength, good elasticity and resilience, and good abrasion resistance. It is relatively lightweight and can be made into very light, sheer, yet strong fabrics. Its strength and quick-drying properties, together with increased wet strength, make it a good choice for outerwear and swimwear.

Nylon's poor moisture absorbency can make the wearer hot in warm temperatures and cold in cool temperatures. This property also causes static build-up and makes nylon difficult to dye. However, it has a higher moisture regain than most other man-made fibers.

Nylon can be heat-set for dimensional stability and with permanent creases and pleats. At low to moderate laundering temperatures, it neither shrinks nor stretches out of shape. It has a tendency to gray and yellow with age. Do not use chlorine bleach. The fiber is degraded by long exposure to sunlight.

Nylon blends well with other fibers; 15 to 20 percent nylon will give added strength to most fabrics.

Antron

Antron is one of the trade names for a variation on nylon, which are claimed to have increased wicking properties. These have a crisper hand, being somewhat more like silk in feel, and have increased luster.

Qiana

Qiana, made by DuPont, has a soft and luxurious hand combined with easy care. It can be laundered and dry cleaned, has good wrinkle resistance and wrinkle recovery. Good wickability compensates somewhat for its low absorbency. The special shape enhances luster and it can be dyed into clear colors with good color fastness.

Aramids

Aramids, including Nomex and Kevlar, have the outstanding property of being temperature and flame resistant. They do not melt and have very low combustibility. Widely used in protective, industrial, military, and sports clothing, their other characteristics include high strength, good flexibility, good abrasion resistance. They do not shrink or stretch.

Polyester

Polyester, first commercially produced in 1953, is one of the most ubiquitous and versatile of man-made fibers. It is a very strong (only nylon is as strong) fiber, dimensionally stable and abrasion resistant, with good elasticity and excellent resilience. For this reason, polyesters are often blended with less crease-resistant fibers to make "easy care" fabrics that require little or no ironing. In wool blends, at least 40 percent polyester must be used to impart this quality; at least 25 percent in rayon blends. Polyester/cotton blends and some 100 percent knitted polyester fibers have a bad tendency to pill.

Polyester is nonwater-absorbent but, in some fabric constructions, it does have a wicking ability. In wicking, the moisture is carried on the surface of the fiber without being absorbed. Thus, perspiration is carried to the surface of the fiber and evaporated, making some polyester fibers, especially in blends, relatively comfortable to wear in warm weather.

Polyester can be laundered or dry cleaned, and can be bleached. However, it absorbs and tenaciously holds oily stains and soil which must be pretreated to be removed. Polyester has good resistance to sunlight.

Acrylic

Acrylic fibers are relatively strong, with good resiliency and high bulking power but their abrasion resistance is only moderate and elasticity is generally lower than other man-mades.

Acrylics have poor moisture absorbency and as a result, tend to build up static electricity. Their woollike hand and bulk, combined with light weight and wrinkle resistance, make them popular for warm, bulky clothing such as sweaters. They drape well and can be dyed with bright colors or muted hues, with a soft luster. They blend well with other fibers, particularly wool and rayon. When blended with at least 50 percent wool, these fabrics can be given a durable pleat or crease.

Acrylics are heat sensitive so instructions on care labels should be followed carefully in laundering. In general, they can be laundered and dry cleaned. Low heat settings for dryer and iron should be used.

Modacrylic

Modacrylics, used largely to make pile, fake fur, and fleece fabrics, are generally slightly weaker than acrylics but their high resilience, combined with good abrasion resistance, makes them especially suitable for use in high pile fabrics. Elastic recovery is good. Their melting point is low, so very low ironing temperatures and no-heat settings on the dryer should be used. In terms of safety, however, they are inherently flame retardant; although they will burn when placed in direct flame, they self-extinguish as soon as the flame is removed.

Spandex

Spandex fibers are of the same composition as polyurethane foam used for mattresses and pillows. Spandex, although twice as strong as rubber, is still relatively weak but it will stretch 500 to 600 percent without breaking. Absorbency is low but water will penetrate, making it easy to dye.

It can be safely dried in a dryer but high laundering and drying temperatures tend to degrade and yellow spandex. Chlorine bleach should not be used.

Spandex is always used in combination with other fibers.

Care and Cleaning

LAUNDERING

There are no absolutes in laundering. No two people wash their clothes exactly the same way: The degree of water hardness and water temperatures vary greatly; different detergents and fabrics and types of soil all contribute to the many variables. However, there are certain basic concepts to apply and experiment with to obtain good results.

How much detergent should you use? Well, according to Maytag, which has one of the best consumer information departments we've had the pleasure to run across, most laundry problems are caused by using *too little* detergent. So follow the instructions on the detergent package. At least with respect to the major name brands, they have actually been carefully formulated and are honestly not calculated to make you use more than you need. However, the quantities given are for the average washload. If your clothes are particularly soiled, use more detergent. Similarly, if your water hardness exceeds the average 5 grains, use additional detergent.

Hard water contains minerals that will interfere with the detergent's ability to clean. (The water department of your municipal government can tell you how hard the water in your area is.) If you find you have a hard water problem, and no water conditioning equipment, a packaged water softener such as Calgon or Spring Rain can be added to both the wash and the rinse water. (NOTE: *Do not mix fabric softeners with water softeners.*) Precipitating water softeners, such as washing soda or sodium carbonate, should be avoided because they form a residue that can cling to fabrics.

As a general rule, the hotter the water, the cleaner your clothes will come out. So use the hottest water that is safe for the fabrics. Detergents and soaps clean best in hot water and become less effective as water temperature decreases until, below 60° F, they are essentially ineffective. If for whatever reason you do not use hot water, then a liquid detergent is recommended because powders will not dissolve as readily. Or you can predissolve powders in a little hot water before adding it to your washload.

Although the best cleaning can be achieved in hot water, many clothes require warm or even cool water because of fiber content, fiber finishes, or for color preservation. Cool water lessens the danger of shrinkage, particularly with knitted fabrics and prevents the "setting" of certain types of stains, such as milk, egg, blood, and other protein soils that can become permanent if washed in hot water. Cool water does, of course, save energy.

Special cool-water detergents have been developed which dissolve readily and clean adequately in cold water. However, even these are more effective in warm or hot water. Pretreating soiled areas will help to compensate for not using hot water.

If you do use cold water, it may be a good idea to check the water temperature with a thermometer. Temperatures for unheated wash water can range from near freezing in Northern areas during the winter to near 100° F in warmer climes during the summer. For best results, temperatures should be no lower than 80° F.

LAUNDRY INGREDIENTS

Both soap and detergent will clean soiled clothes but each should be used in its proper place. The box or bottle should clearly state whether the product is a soap or a detergent.

If the water in your area is hard, soap products have a major drawback: they combine with water hardness minerals to form soap curd or lime curd, an insoluble sticky residue. This curd picks up soil from the wash water and the combination sticks to whatever it comes in contact with (that is, your clothes and the wash basket) and clothes eventually become dingy, gray and greasy-feeling. The addition of a water softener can improve results somewhat.

Synthetic detergents, which came into use after World War II, do not form a curd in hard water and now make up about 95 percent of laundry washing products. All home laundry detergents contain the same basic ingredients: a *surfactant,* which breaks the surface tension of the fabric, allowing water to penetrate, and which also holds the loosened particles of dirt in suspension; a *builder,* which acts as a water softener; and *brighteners,* fluorescent dyes added to make whites look whiter and colors brighter.

Some detergents also contain *enzymes,* which break down complex substances into a more soluble form so they can be washed out.

One of the ingredients that made detergents so successful is phosphate, which is unexcelled as a water softener and also helps to disperse dirt. Now phosphates have been banned in many areas, however, and their levels reduced in all detergents because they were suspected of being a serious contributor to eutrophication or excessive and harmful algal growth in lakes, rivers, and streams. However, untreated sewage and fertilizer run-off continue to be the major culprits causing eutrophication.

The public has now been presented with a host of alternative cleaners. The choices include powdered detergents using sodium silicate or sodium carbonate (washing soda); liquid detergents using sodium citrate; or "heavy-duty" liquid detergents formulated without a builder, such as Era or Dynamo, which utilize a surfactant insensitive to interference by water hardness.

With liquid detergents, whether the "heavy-duty" type or sodium citrate type, you will probably notice little if any difference in their performance compared with phosphate detergents.

However, phosphate-free *powdered* detergents, which are the most common, present some drawbacks. They may not get clothes as clean; may make them feel harsh and scratchy; may cause color loss or change; and may react with hardness minerals to deposit a residue, often mistaken for lint, on your clothes. This is because sodium carbonate works as a precipitating water softener. The resulting precipitate can build up on your clothes and the washing machine, causing all of the above-mentioned problems. Sodium carbonate can also cause an adverse effect on the durability and aesthetic properties of chemical finishes, such as durable press, soil release, and water repellency. Some studies have shown that, used in hard water, sodium carbonate detergents can reduce garments' wear life.

If for some reason you must use a sodium carbonate detergent, use the hottest water suitable for the clothes and thoroughly dissolve the detergent in the water before adding your clothes.

If a lintlike residue does build up on your clothes, this can sometimes be removed by soaking in a mild acid such as vinegar. Use one cup vinegar to one gallon water. Do NOT soak in the washing machine because this can damage it. Before taking this step, check for color fastness against acid on a hidden area. For extra softness, follow the treatment with a fabric softener.

CAUTION: *Cotton clothes with a flame retardant finish should never be washed in sodium carbonate detergents if you have hard water.* No flame retardant garment—cotton or synthetic—should be washed in soap. Use phosphate detergent or phosphate-free liquid silicate detergents only.

FABRIC SOFTENERS

When detergents, which contain no fats, largely replaced soaps, which leave a fatty residue on clothes making them feel soft, the detergent industry developed fabric softeners.

Fabric softeners do a lot more than just make fabrics feel softer. They reduce or eliminate static cling in man-made fabrics; make some fabrics fluffier; reduce wrinkling in an automatic dryer and facilitate ironing; and they help to prevent lint from sticking to garments. An interesting side effect determined by the J. C. Penney Company is that fabric softeners can substantially improve the tear and abrasion resistance of fabrics by acting as a fabric lubricant. Basically, the fabric softener coats the fiber strands with a lubricating film which allows the fibers to move more freely against each other.

Follow label instructions carefully. Keep in mind that fabric softeners are absorbed by the fabrics, therefore the amount used should be adjusted to the size of the clothes load, not to the amount of water in the tub. Too much softener will cause clothes to look yellow and dingy, to feel greasy, and be nonabsorbent. Because softeners can reduce absorbency, they should be used judiciously on items such as towels and cotton underclothes.

Be careful not to pour undiluted softener directly onto clothes because it can cause an oily, greasy-looking spot which, in subsequent washings, will attract rust and soil from the wash water and come out looking like gray or black grease. To remove such stains, rub the dampened spot with hand soap and rewash.

Fabric softeners are available in three types: rinse-cycle liquid softeners, wash-cycle liquid softeners, and sheet-form dryer-added softeners.

Rinse-cycle softeners are the most effective type and generally the most economical. Unfortunately, they can be inconvenient if your washer is not equipped with an automatic dispenser and you have to remember to add it to the rinse cycle at the right time. Never mix rinse-cycle softeners with detergent or soap, bleach, bluing, or packaged water-softeners. Any of these mixed with the fabric softener will react to make both ineffective and will deposit a white, sticky residue all over your clothes. Use only as directed— in the final rinse and by itself.

BLEACHES

Bleach has increased in importance recently for several reasons. Man-made fabrics have an affinity for oily types of soil and more cleaning power is often necessary to prevent soil build-up. Because of the reduced power of no-phosphate detergents and of cold water washing, bleach is being used as a booster.

Liquid chlorine bleach is the most popular and also the most powerful and therefore potentially most destructive to fabrics and colors. Improperly used, it can cause serious fabric damage and color change. Be particularly careful with the cellulosic fibers: cotton, linen, rayon, acetate, and triacetate. When full-strength bleach comes into direct contact with these fabrics, it weakens them. Although damage may not appear until several launderings later, it is likely to show up as rips, tears, or holes.

Bleach, even if diluted, should *never* be used on wool, mohair, down, silk, spandex, or fabrics that contain even a small percentage of these fibers because bleach will permanently damage them. It should also never be used on noncolorfast colors or on certain flame retardant finishes, especially those on 100 percent cotton garments. Check labels carefully.

Generally speaking, all man-made fibers (except spandex) and durable press finishes can be bleached with liquid chlorine bleach (unless the care label states otherwise). In addition, many colors can be safely chlorine bleached. To check for color fastness, mix 1 tablespoon bleach with 1/4 cup of water. Apply a drop to a hidden area of the garment. Make sure the solution penetrates and let stand one minute. Then blot dry with a white paper towel. If there is no color change, it can be safely bleached. Be sure to dilute the bleach correctly before using; we would recommend erring on the side of an overly weak solution.

Powdered chlorine bleach is milder than the liquid form and releases bleaching ingredients more slowly as it dissolves, but it too can damage clothes if improperly used. Never sprinkle directly on clothes.

Oxygen bleaches, so-called because they release oxygen rather than chlorine, are generally safer for all washable fabrics. They produce little if any damage to fabrics and are less damaging to colors, nor will they yellow chlorine-retentive finishes and fibers. Because their reaction is milder, however, their stain removal ability is limited and they cannot restore whiteness to the same degree as chlorine bleaches. They are most effective when used consistently.

When using any kind of bleach, always follow directions carefully. Never pour bleach, whether liquid or powdered, directly on clothes; mix well with water first. Quantities stated on the container are the *maximum;* they should never be exceeded.

WHY FABRICS SHRINK

Yarns and fabrics are stretched and placed under great tension during their manufacture. When the material is wetted during laundering, this tension is relaxed and thus the garment shrinks. This is known as relaxation shrinkage and it will usually take two to five washings to fully shrink a garment, although the majority of the shrinkage will occur in the first washing. Some manufacturers offer preshrunk and stabilized fabrics which, although the cost is higher, can be a worthwhile investment. These fabrics will still have some residual shrinkage but it is relatively minor.

Fabrics generally shrink more in their length than their width. Because far more tension is exerted on the warp or lengthwise yarns during weaving than on the filling yarns, their relaxation will be proportionately greater.

The mechanical action of washing machines and particularly dryers when high heat is used causes another type of shrinkage which results from a distorted fiber returning to its natural shape. This type of shrinkage does not happen with hand-washing and dry cleaning. Often a fiber becomes shorter and wider, so the bulk may actually increase, whereas the length decreases. This has the side effect of making the weave tighter, but this may be small comfort if your garment no longer fits.

Dry cleaning generally does not cause shrinkage, although shrinkage can occur if there is a high moisture content in the solvent or from steaming during pressing.

A number of shrinkage control processes have been developed, including the commonly recognized trademarks of the Sanforized company. Equally effective processes can be used on knits. The term *preshrunk* does not mean the garment will shrink no more, just that much of the shrinkage potential has been removed. In our opinion, to have proven its worth, a preshrunk garment should never shrink out of fit. If it does, you've been ripped off.

Cheaper untreated fabrics are likely to shrink more than a better quality, carefully woven textile.

Felting shrinkage may occur in wool and hair fibers which, because of their scaly surface, have a natural tendency to shorten and mat together. This same characteristic is employed in making felt. Once a fabric has become felted, it is impossible to stretch it back to its original size.

Felting can be caused by excessive mechanical action during cleaning and drying; high temperatures together with tumbling action in drying; and high relative humidity of the solvent during dry cleaning. Recommended dry-cleaning plant practices or hand-washing procedures will usually control this problem.

Soft, loosely woven woolen fabrics will felt more than hard finished wool or worsted fabrics.

MACHINE WASHING

Sort laundry carefully according to color, degree of soil, and delicacy of construction. Separate whites from colors and light colors from dark colors. White durable press and synthetic fabrics, especially nylon, should be washed only with other whites because they are most prone to discoloration.

Some fabrics, such as white cottons, linens, and underwear, may need hot water and vigorous washing; others, such as washable woolens and dark colors, require cooler water and short wash times to prevent shrinkage and fading. Some durable press and man-made fabrics require special treatment to prevent wrinkling.

Keep heavily soiled garments and lightly soiled clothes

separated, because the lightly soiled ones may suffer from redeposition of soil from the dirtier clothes.

Loosely knit garments, hand washables, and articles with lace trim should be washed on a Delicate cycle, not with your work clothes. Keep fabrics that lint, such as terry cloth, chenille, and bath towels separate from fabrics that attract lint, such as corduroy, velveteen, man-made, and durable press fabrics. Light-colored lint producers in particular can wreak havoc on dark-colored lint attractors.

Make up each load with articles of differing sizes to allow free circulation in the water; no more than two or three sheets, or similar large articles, should be included, with smaller articles added to round out the load.

Empty all pockets. Shake out loose dirt and brush lint from trouser cuffs. Make necessary repairs before laundering—any rips and tears will probably worsen with washing. Close zippers, hooks, and eyes so they do not snag on other clothes.

Pretreat stains (see Stain Removal, pp. 183–186) and heavy soil on collars, knees, and cuffs with a liquid detergent or prewash spray applied directly to the soiled area. (Spray prewash products can remove markings from dials and buttons on some washing machines and may soften fingernail polish, so exercise caution.) Before pretreating, check color sensitivity by rubbing a paste of your prewash product or concentrated detergent on a hidden area. Rinse and check for color change.

Color loss in laundering should be minimal; severe color loss should not be tolerated—return the garment.

Now for the actual washing. IMPORTANT: *Do not overload the washer.* Clothes won't wash as clean and overloading also causes excessive wear on your clothes. Subdivide your piles into smaller ones, if necessary.

Follow package directions for the recommended amount of detergent to use. These are recommendations for "average" washing conditions, however. Extra detergent should be used for a big load, very dirty clothes, maximum water levels, or in hard water. Similarly, use less detergent for small loads, lightly soiled clothes, partial water levels, and soft water.

To thoroughly disperse detergent in the water and to avoid the risk of pouring detergent and other cleaning agents directly onto clothes, first partially fill the washer with water, then stop the machine, measure in the detergent, and stir it around before adding your clothes. This method, naturally, is not advised for front loading machines, unless of course you want to flood your home.

DRYING

First, make sure the lint filter is clean.

Do not overload the dryer; this will lengthen drying time, result in uneven drying, and cause unnecessary wrinkling. Clothes need room to tumble. As in washing, fabrics of similar color should be dried together; it is possible for colors to run from one fabric to another while damp. Equally, do not mix lint producers with lint attractors.

Commercial coin-operated dryers tend to run a lot hotter, even on lower settings, than regular home dryers so be careful, especially with heat-sensitive fabrics. These should be dried at low heat or no heat settings. Consult care labels. Olefins are extremely heat sensitive. Elastics made with natural rubber can lose their elasticity over a period of time if repeatedly dried in a hot dryer. Items containing foam rubber or foam rubberlike materials must never be dried on a heat setting. When heated, these materials can, under certain circumstances, produce fire by spontaneous combustion.

Take clothes out of the dryer before they are "bone dry." If they get too dry, they wrinkle, feel stiff, and some may shrink. It is normal for elastic bands in underpants, bras, and socks to feel slightly damp when first removed from the dryer. Durable press and man-made fabrics should be removed from the dryer immediately upon completion of the cycle to prevent the setting of wrinkles. This is a good practice for any fabrics, to reduce wrinkling.

HAND WASHING

Woolens that are not labeled machine washable should be either hand washed or dry cleaned. Hand wash any clothes with non-colorfast colors, with seams that may fray or pull apart, or with any special finishes or ornamentation that may require careful handling. As a general rule, when in doubt, hand wash (or dry clean).

Water temperature should be about 80° F and feel tepid to the hand. Even cold-water detergents are more effective when water temperature is around 80° F or more. Soft water is preferable but if water is hard, a water softener can be added before the soap, or a mild detergent can be used.

Completely dissolve the soap or detergent before adding clothes and then gently squeeze the suds through the clothes.

Rinse several times, each time in fresh water. A water softener should be added to the rinse water as well if water is hard. Once the water rinses clean, squeeze out—do not wring out—excess water, then roll the garment in a bath towel and gently press out additional water. Always support wools from underneath when you lift them out of the water. Drip-dry fabrics should just be hung on a rustproof hanger, without any squeezing.

If colors have a tendency to run, clothes should be rinsed often until the rinse water looks clear. Then hang in front of a fan or in a breeze so the garment will dry quickly.

Generally, garments made with woven fabrics can be hung to dry on rounded, rustproof hangers. Knits should be laid out flat, to avoid stretching out of shape.

IRONING

Fabrics are best pressed while still slightly damp, or using steam, because wrinkles will be more easily removed. Linens and cottons require the highest temperatures; man-mades the lowest. Some durable press and man-made fabrics may require little or no ironing.

Be sure to read labels carefully for correct ironing temperature. Blends should always be ironed at a heat setting suitable for the fiber requiring the lower heat. For example, a blend of polyester and cotton should be ironed at the setting for polyester, not cotton.

Silks, rayons, acetates, and all dark-colored fabrics should be pressed on the wrong side to avoid shine. If they must be pressed on the right side, use a press cloth.

Wool fabrics should be ironed with steam on the wrong side or with a dampened press cloth. Dry heat can damage wool. Lower and lift the iron; don't slide it back and forth. Prevent imprinting from inside detail by placing tissues, wrapping paper, or the like under folds, seams, and darts.

Silk should be pressed with a dry press cloth because it can water-spot. For this reason, use caution with steam.

Napped or textured surfaced fabrics should be tested carefully to see if pressing will flatten the surface. Sometimes they can be successfully pressed on the wrong side, using a terry towel or other soft surface underneath. Special pressing boards, called needle boards, are best for corduroys and velvets. These fabrics also may respond well to steam or to being hung in a bathroom still warm and humid from a hot shower. To steam, pass a steam iron or "wrinkle remover" steamer several inches away from the garment, then hang to dry to allow wrinkles to fall out.

STAIN REMOVAL

Stain removal is easiest when the stain is dealt with immediately. Some stains may be initially invisible when fresh, until heat from drying and pressing turns them brown. Once set, they can rarely be removed. Such stains can be caused by the sugar in fruit juices, artificially sweetened soft drinks, ginger ale, and cocktails. Flush with cool water immediately while still fresh.

Before using a stain remover, first test for color fastness by sponging a small amount of the remover on a seam or hem. Stains of unknown origin and stains on certain delicate or Dry Clean Only fabrics are best treated by a dry cleaner.

Enzyme presoaks are especially effective for protein-based stains caused by body soils, blood, egg, grass, and chocolate. Soak 30 minutes to overnight, depending on age and amount of stain. These are not effective if used during laundering.

Spray-on prewash soil and stain removers that contain perchloroethylene or other petroleum-based solvents are good on man-made and durable press fabrics for removing greasy stains. Some may dissolve markings on washing machine buttons and dials, and may soften paint and fingernail polish, so use carefully.

Removing Greasy Stains

If the fabric is washable, first try rubbing soap or detergent into the stain, then rinse with warm water. Most likely, you will have to use a grease solvent. Use in a well-ventilated room, away from any source of flame or sparks, and avoid inhaling the fumes. After testing for colorfastness on a hidden area, place the fabric, wrong side up, over a pad of clean, absorbent, white cotton fabric or paper towel. Then sponge the stain throughly with solvent.

If stains have been set by heat or age, a yellow discoloration may remain. If the fabric is washable and safe to bleach, chlorine or perborate bleach may remove this color.

Removing Nongreasy Stains

Stains set by age or heat may be very difficult to remove. Sponge or soak washable items with cool water. If the stain persists, rub a little soap or detergent on the spot, then rinse. If this is not successful, try bleach if the fabric can be bleached.

Nonwashable clothes can sometimes be safely sponged with cool water. If necessary, rub in a little detergent. To rinse without wetting a large area of the fabric, place an absorbent material underneath, and use a small syringe to force water through the cloth. A final sponging with alcohol can help to remove any remaining detergent. Fabrics should first be tested for colorfastness to alcohol. On acetates, use only alcohol diluted with two parts of water.

Removing Combination Stains

Because these stains combine greasy and nongreasy ingredients, both methods of removal must be used. First sponge with cool water. Then treat with detergent, rinse, and dry. Treat any remaining greasy stains with a grease solvent. Stubborn stains may require bleaching.

STAIN REMOVAL GUIDE*

This chart applies only to washable items. It does not apply to garments which should be dry-cleaned. Some stains are not easily seen when the fabric is wet. Air-dry the articles to be certain the stain has been removed. Machine drying might make the stain more difficult to remove. Prewash products may be more convenient to use in treating stains than the process of rubbing detergent into the dampened stain.

	BLEACHABLE FABRICS: White and colorfast cotton, linen, polyester, acrylic, triacetate, nylon, rayon, permanent press	**NON-BLEACHABLE FABRICS:** Wool, silk, spandex, noncolorfast items, some flame retardant finishes (check labels)
Stain	**Removal procedure for washable garments.**	**Removal procedure for washable garments.**
Alcoholic beverages	Sponge stain promptly with cold water or soak in cold water for 30 minutes or longer. Rub detergent into any remaining stain while still wet. Launder in hot water using chlorine bleach.	Sponge stain promptly with cold water or soak in cold water for 30 minutes or longer. Sponge with vinegar. Rinse. If stain remains, rub detergent into stain. Rinse. Launder.
Blood	Soak in cold water 30 minutes or longer. Rub detergent into any remaining stain. Rinse. If stain persists, put a few drops of ammonia on the stain and repeat detergent treatment. Rinse. If stain still persists, launder in hot water using chlorine bleach.	Same method, but if colorfastness is questionable, use hydrogen peroxide** instead of ammonia. Launder in warm water. Omit chlorine bleach.
Candle wax	Rub with ice cube to harden wax and then carefully scrape off wax with dull knife. Place between several layers of facial tissue or paper towels and press with a warm iron. Replace towels frequently to absorb more wax. To remove remaining stain, place face down on clean paper towels and sponge with dry-cleaning fluid. If colored stain remains, launder in hot water using chlorine bleach. Launder again if necessary.	Same method. Launder in warm water. Omit chlorine bleach.
Carbon paper	Rub detergent into dampened stain; rinse well. If stain is not removed, put a few drops of ammonia on the stain and repeat treatment with detergent; rinse well. Repeat if necessary.	Same method, but if colorfastness is questionable, use hydrogen peroxide** instead of ammonia.
Catsup	Scrape off excess with a dull knife. Soak in cold water 30 minutes. Rub detergent into stain while still wet and launder in hot water using chlorine bleach.	Same method. Launder in warm water. Omit chlorine bleach.
Chewing gum, adhesive tape	Rub stained area with ice. Remove excess gummy matter carefully with a dull knife. Place face down on paper towels and sponge with a safe cleaning fluid. Rinse and launder.	Same method.
Chocolate and cocoa	Soak in cold water. Rub detergent into stain while still wet, then rinse thoroughly. Dry. If a greasy stain remains, sponge with a safe cleaning fluid. Rinse. Launder in hot water using chlorine bleach. If stain remains, repeat treatment with cleaning fluid.	Same method. Launder in warm water. Omit chlorine bleach.
Coffee, tea	Soak in cold water. Rub detergent into stain while still wet. Rinse and dry. If grease stain remains from cream, sponge with safe cleaning fluid. Launder in hot water using chlorine bleach.	Same method. Launder in warm water. Omit chlorine bleach.
Cosmetics (eye shadow, lipstick, liquid makeup, mascara, powder, rouge)	Rub detergent into dampened stain until outline of stain is gone, then rinse well. Launder in hot water using chlorine bleach.	Same method. Launder in warm water. Omit chlorine bleach.
Crayon	Rub soap into dampened stain, working until outline of stain is removed. Launder in hot water using chlorine bleach. Repeat process if necessary.	Same method. Launder in warm water using plenty of detergent. Omit chlorine bleach.
Deodorants and antiperspirants	Rub detergent into dampened stain. Launder in hot water using chlorine bleach. Antiperspirants that contain such substances as aluminum chloride are acidic and may change the color of some dyes. Color may or may not be restored by sponging with ammonia. Rinse thoroughly.	Rub detergent into dampened stain. Launder in warm water. Antiperspirants that contain such substances as aluminum chloride are acidic and may change the color of some dyes. Color may or may not be restored by sponging with ammonia. (If ammonia treatment is required, dilute with an equal amount of water for use on wool, mohair, or silk.) Rinse thoroughly.

*Based on information supplied by The Maytag Company and Proctor and Gamble. Used with permission.
**Available at drugstore.

	BLEACHABLE FABRICS: White and colorfast cotton, linen, polyester, acrylic, triacetate, nylon, rayon, permanent press	**NON-BLEACHABLE FABRICS:** Wool, silk, spandex, noncolorfast items, some flame retardant finishes (check labels)
Stain	**Removal procedure for washable garments.**	**Removal procedure for washable garments.**
Dye (transferred from a noncolorfast article)	May be impossible to remove. Bleach immediately using chlorine bleach. Repeat as often as necessary. Or use a commercial color remover	Use a commercial color remover.
Egg, meat juice, and gravy	If dried, scrape off as much as possible with a dull knife. Soak in cold water. Rub detergent into stain while still wet. Launder in hot water using chlorine bleach.	Same method. Launder in warm water. Omit chlorine bleach.
Fabric softener	Rub the dampened stain with hand soap and relaunder in the usual manner.	Same method.
Fingernail polish	Place stain face down on paper towels. Sponge white cotton fabric with nail polish remover; other fabrics with amyl acetate** (banana oil). Launder. Repeat if necessary.	Same method.
Fruit juices	Soak in cold water. Launder in hot water using chlorine bleach.	Soak in cold water. If stain remains, rub detergent into stain while still wet. Launder in warm water.
Grass	Rub detergent into dampened stain. Launder in hot water using chlorine bleach. If stain remains, sponge with alcohol. Rinse thoroughly.	Same method. Launder in warm water. Omit chlorine bleach. If colorfastness is questionable or fabric is acetate, dilute alcohol with two parts water.
Grease and oil (car grease, butter, shortening, oily medicines such as oily vitamins)	Rub detergent into dampened stain. Launder in hot water using chlorine bleach and plenty of detergent. If stain persists, sponge thoroughly with safe cleaning fluid. Rinse.	Rub detergent into dampened stain. Launder in warm water using plenty of detergent. If stain persists, sponge thoroughly with safe cleaning fluid. Rinse.
Ink, ballpoint	Sponge stain with rubbing alcohol, or spray with hair spray until wet looking. Rub detergent into stained area. Launder. Repeat if necessary.	Same method.
Ink, drawing	May be impossible to remove. Run cold water through stain until no more color is being removed. Rub detergent into stain, rinse. Repeat if necessary. Soak in warm sudsy water containing one to four tablespoons of ammonia to a quart of water. Rinse thoroughly. Launder in hot water using chlorine bleach.	Same method. Launder in warm water. Omit chlorine bleach.
Ink from felt tip pen	Rub liquid household cleaner into stain. Rinse. Repeat as many times as necessary to remove stain. Launder. Some may be impossible to remove.	Same method.
Iodine	Rinse from underside of stain with cool water. Soak in solution of color remover. Rinse and launder.	Same method.
Mayonnaise, salad dressing	Rub detergent into dampened stain. Rinse and let dry. If greasy stain remains, sponge with safe cleaning fluid. Rinse. Launder in hot water with chlorine bleach.	Same method. Launder in warm water. Omit chlorine bleach.
Mildew	Rub detergent into dampened stain. Launder in hot water using chlorine bleach. If stain remains, sponge with hydrogen peroxide.** Rinse and launder.	Same method. Launder in warm water. Omit chlorine bleach.
Milk, cream, ice cream	Soak in cold water. Launder in hot water using chlorine bleach. If grease stain remains, sponge with safe cleaning fluid. Rinse.	Soak in cold water. Rub detergent into stain. Launder. If grease stain remains, sponge with safe cleaning fluid. Rinse.
Mustard	Rub detergent into dampened stain. Rinse. Soak in hot detergent water for several hours. If stain remains, launder in hot water using chlorine bleach.	Same method. Launder in warm water. Omit chlorine bleach.
Paint and varnish	Treat stains quickly before paint dries. If a solvent is recommended as a thinner, sponge it onto stain. Turpentine or trichloroethane can be used. While stain is still wet with solvent, work detergent into stain and soak in hot water. Then launder. Repeat procedure if stain remains after laundering. Stain may be impossible to remove. For latex, acrylic, (cont.)	Same method.

	BLEACHABLE FABRICS: White and colorfast cotton, linen, polyester, acrylic, triacetate, nylon, rayon, permanent press	**NON-BLEACHABLE FABRICS:** Wool, silk, spandex, noncolorfast items, some flame retardant finishes (check labels)
Stain	Removal procedure for washable garments.	Removal procedure for washable garments.
Paint and varnish (cont.)	and waterbase paints, rinse in warm water to flush out paint, then launder. These stains must be treated while still wet; they cannot be removed once they have dried.	
Perfume	Same as alcoholic beverages.	Same as alcoholic beverages.
Perspiration	Rub detergent into dampened stain. Launder in hot water using chlorine bleach. If fabric has discolored, try to restore it by treating fresh stains with ammonia or old stains with vinegar. Rinse. Launder.	Same method. Launder in warm water. Omit chlorine bleach.
Ring around the collar	Apply liquid laundry detergent or a paste of granular detergent and water on the stain. Let it set for 30 minutes. A prewash product especially designed for this purpose may be used. Follow manufacturer's directions. Launder.	Same method.
Rust Few spots Rusty discoloration on load of white items	Do not use chlorine bleach on rust. Apply a rust stain remover. Rinse and launder. Wash in phosphate detergent, if available, with one cup of an oxygen bleach. If stains remain, dissolve 1 ounce oxalic acid crystals per gallon of water in a plastic container. Soak clothes for 10–15 minutes. Rinse and launder.	Same method. If colorfastness is questionable, test a concealed area first.
Scorch	Launder in hot water using chlorine bleach or rust remover. Severe scorching cannot be removed; fabric has been damaged.	Cover stains with cloth dampened with hydrogen peroxide. Cover with a dry cloth and press with an iron as hot as is safe for fabric. Rinse thoroughly. Rub detergent into stained area while still wet. Launder. Repeat if necessary.
Shoe polish (wax)	Scrape off as much as possible with a dull knife. Rub detergent into dampened stain. Launder in hot water using chlorine bleach. If stain persists, sponge with rubbing alcohol. Rinse. Launder.	Scrape off as much as possible with a dull knife. Rub detergent into dampened stain. Launder in warm water. If stain persists, sponge with one part alcohol and two parts water. Rinse. Launder.
Soft drinks	Sponge stain immediately with cold water. Launder in hot water with chlorine bleach. Some drink stains are invisible after they dry, but turn yellow with aging or heating. This yellow stain may be impossible to remove.	Same method. Launder in warm water. Omit chlorine bleach.
Tar and asphalt	Act quickly before stain is dry. Pour trichloroethane through cloth. Repeat. Stain may be impossible to remove. Rinse and launder.	Same method.
Urine	Soak in cold water. Rub detergent into stain. Launder in hot water using chlorine bleach. If the color of the fabric has been altered by stain, sponge with ammonia; rinse thoroughly. If stain persists, sponging with vinegar may help.	Same method. Launder in warm water. Omit chlorine bleach. If ammonia treatment is necessary, dilute ammonia with an equal part of water for use on wool, mohair, or silk.
Wine	Same treatment as for alcoholic beverages. Wait 15 minutes and rinse. Repeat if necessary.	Same treatment as for alcoholic beverages.
Yellowing of white cottons and linens	Use a color remover. Dissolve remover in cold water. Fill machine with hot water, add color remover and clothes. Alternately agitate and soak 30 minutes. Let washer complete cycle OR fill washer with very hot water. Add at least twice as much detergent as normal. Place articles in washer and agitate for four minutes at regular speed. Stop washer and add one cup of chlorine bleach diluted in one quart of water by pouring around agitator. Restart washer at once. Agitate four minutes. Stop washer and allow articles to soak 15 minutes. Restart washer and set ten minute wash time; allow washer to complete normal cycle. Repeat entire procedure two or more consecutive times until whiteness is restored.	
Yellowing of white nylon, polyester, and durable press	Soak 15 to 30 minutes in solution of 1/8 cup of liquid chlorine bleach and one teaspoon of vinegar thoroughly mixed with each gallon of warm water. Rinse. Repeat if necessary.	

DRY CLEANING

Dry cleaning is a highly technical skill. It cannot be learned properly in a short period of time but must be carefully studied and mastered. As the textile and fabric finishing industries constantly develop new products or variations on old ones, the dry cleaner's skill is challenged as new cleaning techniques must be employed.

There are many responsible, reliable, and highly qualified dry cleaners in this country. Unfortunately, as many of us have learned to our dismay, there are also many poor dry cleaners. The challenge to the consumer is to distinguish one from the other *before* risking a cherished garment. This is very difficult.

A number of experts we've consulted, including dry cleaners, have compared finding a good cleaner with finding a lawyer or a doctor. The areas that distinguish the good from the bad are ones that the customer can seldom query or determine in advance, before having to find out by trial and error. The first rule of thumb is, never take a favorite or irreplaceable or very delicate garment to a dry cleaner you are trying out for the first time. Take something that can stand up to some possible mishandling.

A dry cleaner who belongs to a trade association, such as International Fabricare Institute, is more likely to be up to date on the latest technical information. Of course, even if the cleaner receives information, it still has to be read and understood before it can do any good.

Another way to distinguish good from bad is to ask people in your neighborhood who you feel would have standards of care similar to your own.

Some of the most common dry-cleaning complaints are the use of dirty fluid, which not only redeposits dirt but also leaves a smell on your clothes and makes them look dingy and dull; pressing double creases in trousers; incorrect removal or failure to remove stains. It must be added here, in all fairness, that the faster you take stained clothes to the cleaners, the better a chance they have of removing the stains.

Many garments labeled dry-cleanable are in fact not. This is not the dry cleaner's fault; it is the manufacturer's responsibility. An experienced dry cleaner may in some cases be able to tell in advance when a garment cannot be dry cleaned and should decline to accept it. If a garment is damaged by dry cleaning through no fault of the cleaner's, and it is clearly labeled dry-cleanable, the manufacturer should be contacted, either through the retailer or directly, the problem explained, and satisfaction obtained if possible. This can be a long and arduous process but one that should be carried out. Such failure of serviceability is most likely to occur in very fashionable clothing, where the "look" is more important than serviceability.

Be smart: Bring your clothes to the dry cleaner neatly folded. If you bring in rumpled shirts, pants, jackets that look as though they've been thrown in a heap on the floor for the past week (as they may well have been), it shows a lack of concern for your clothes and you could be influencing the cleaner into taking the same attitude. Also, this is just not good for clothes. For example, a good suit jacket's inner construction is often made of horsehair to give it shape. If this lining is repeatedly bent, it will eventually break, and the jacket will lose its shape.

Loose buttons and other needed minor repairs as well as stains should be pointed out to the cleaner.

Incidentally, clothes should not be sent to the cleaner's just for pressing without first being cleaned. This presses in dirt and grit, which act as abrasives, and the heat of pressing sets any stains, making them far more difficult, if not impossible, to remove. Allowing your clothes a rest between wearings will give wrinkles time to hang out. Hanging them in the bathroom during or right after taking a hot shower will also help remove wrinkles because of the warm humid air.

Some dry cleaners offer additional services such as water and stain repellency and mothproofing. Water repellency is accomplished by a coating applied to the fabric to make it shed water, which is also how stain repellents work. Repellency does not render the fabric nonporous and still allows it to "breathe." (It must never be used on down garments.) Repellency, like stain protection, is never a permanent application. When applied by the manufacturer, it will generally last through two or three cleanings. When applied by the cleaner, it will last through one or two cleanings.

CLOTHES STORAGE

For any lengthy storage, clothes must be put away spotlessly clean. Spots that could be easily laundered while fresh may become permanently set with age. Insects will eat food in stained clothing (even if the fiber contains no wool or other natural fibers) and they're not so discriminating that they won't eat the cloth at the same time. Cleaning the clothes will kill any moth larvae already in the garment and a dry cleaner can apply a special mothproofing treatment as well.

Clothes should be stored loosely, not crammed together. When it comes time to unpack your clothes, they will be less wrinkled. Don't store your clothes in plastic; this can create a damp environment and lead to mildewing. Protect with cloth or paper garment bags or fold loosely in drawers or cardboard boxes. Raise boxes off the floor because insects can easily eat their way through cardboard. Store in a cool, dry place, not in a warm closet or attic, and never near a radiator or heat pipe.

Sweaters and knitted garments should always be stored flat. Stuff them with tissue paper so fold marks will not be obvious. The pile on pile fabrics, however, can become permanently distorted when folded for long periods, so extra care must be taken. They can be hung instead on a padded hanger.

Woven garments can either be folded loosely or hung on padded hangers. Close all fastenings so the garment won't hang out of shape. Exceptions to this are garments such as suits or sports jackets, which should be hung unbuttoned. Remove garment belts and either store them flat or hang by the buckle from a hook or the hanger so the backing will not crack.

Insect damage may occur on man-made fabrics if they are dirty or if wool is stored with them; voracious carpet beetles and insidious moth larvae have been known to chew through nonwoolen fabrics to reach the wool underneath.

Have garments mothproofed at the dry cleaner and/or sprinkle a moth preventive into clothes containers and closets. The most common are napthalene and paradichlorobenzene in ball, flake, or disc form, which, if used as directed, are harmless to fabrics. Do not, however, put them in direct contact with clothes—their basic ingredient can set off a chemical reaction with certain dyes, causing discoloration. Also, moth preventives should be kept away from anything plastic because they can soften certain types. Then seal the container to seal in moth killer fumes and keep out moisture.

Contrary to folk mythology, cedar chests and cedar-lined closets do not repel moths and other insects. If moths manage to gain entry, the cedar will not kill them and your clothes will be at their mercy. And those of us who have had experience with these pesky devils know they are without scruples.

Box storage facilities, with controlled temperature and humidity, are also available at some dry cleaners. Furs should be professionally stored. Leathers and suedes can be stored at home in cloth or paper garment bags in a cool, dry, well-ventilated place.

Index